KU-715-722

Decisions at 17/18+

Beryl Dixon

CARDIFF COUNTY COUNCIL
CYNOR SIR CAERDYDD

CENTRAL
LIBRARY

FOR
REFERENCE ONLY

Student Helpbook Series

ACC. No: 02564365

371.425
DIX

Decisions at 17/18+ – sixth edition

Published by Lifetime Careers Publishing, 7 Ascot Court, White Horse Business Park, Trowbridge BA14 0XA

© Lifetime Careers Wiltshire Ltd, 2006

ISBN 1 902876 94 6

ISBN-13 978 190187694 8

No part of this publication may be copied or reproduced, stored in a retrieval system or transmitted in any form or by any means electronic or mechanical or by photocopying or recording without prior permission of the publishers.

Printed and bound by Cromwell Press Ltd, Trowbridge
Cover design by Lesley May
Illustrations by Joe Wright

Contents

About the author

Beryl Dixon is an experienced careers adviser who has worked for different careers companies and in a tertiary college, where she helped students aged 16-19 with their decisions on both higher education and employment. She has also worked for the Ministry of Defence and the Department for Education and Skills, visiting schools in Brussels, Luxembourg, Cyprus and Hong Kong to provide careers advice to the children of expatriate service personnel and government officials.

She now concentrates on careers writing and is the author of several books. She writes regularly on careers and higher education for *The Times* and *The Independent*.

Acknowledgements

I would like to thank Anne Marie Dhillon at the Institute of Legal Executives and the Learning and Skills Council Apprenticeships Team, who provided contact details for some of those who agreed to act as case studies for this book. Thanks also to all the people who appear as case studies.

Chapter one
Where are you now?

Are you at:

■ school or college, doing A levels?

■ college doing a vocational qualification like a National Diploma or professional diploma course, for example leading to the CACHE diploma?

■ in work perhaps – but you've picked up a copy of this book out of curiosity?

■ on an Apprenticeship?

Have you already got qualifications at level 3* and are you ready to take the next step?

Then read on!

Now answer these questions.

1. Have I a clear idea of where I am going?

2. Do I understand what I have to do to get there?

3. Do I have a firm idea about the career I want to do?

4. Have I a clear career idea, but need to know how to get there?

5. Have I no ideas at all?

6. Do I need some ideas?

7. Do I know what the alternatives are?

8. Have I already chosen between education and employment?

* **Please note**: throughout this book, 'level 3' refers to level 3 as specified in the National Qualifications Framework for England (i.e. A levels/NVQ level 3), or the equivalent level in Scotland. Also within the book, where years 11, 12 or 13 are mentioned, this is intended to cover the equivalent year groups in Scotland.

9. Do I want to go on to higher education?

10. Do I need more information about higher education?

11. Do I know what all the different higher-level qualifications are?

12. Do I know which higher education qualifications I could take?

How many times did you answer 'Yes'? Never? Once? Five times or more? Then, this book is for you!

Yes you have read correctly and no, it is not a trick! It is possible to answer 'Yes' to each (although not all) of the individual questions and still be in need of more information. Even if you have a clear idea of where you are going, and know what you have to do to achieve your objective, there may be some detail that you haven't thought of. While you won't find all the information you need in this book, you *will* find some pointers to get you thinking, and to signpost you to further information.

The book isn't intended to be exhaustive, rather to outline and summarise the options that are open to people with level 3 qualifications. There is a mass of information on higher education for example, produced by UCAS and by individual authors. There is even an entire book written on how to complete your UCAS application! To cover everything on these topics in detail would take a library instead of a book! What is different about *Decisions at 17/18+* is that it provides an informative overview of *all* the options at 18 in one single publication (and in a format that you can easily read on the bus or the train!). You can either dip into chapters that particularly interest you, or read it from cover to cover. The book will help you to consider the pros and cons of each route. It may even tempt you to consider an option you have never really thought about before!

Once you are ready to investigate particular options further, information is given as to where to find out more. If you want to learn more about entering employment, another book in this series, *Jobs and careers after A levels & equivalent advanced qualifications* can take you further. A large part of that book consists of case studies of people who are at work, and describes the work that they do and the training they are receiving.

Use the following questions to guide you to the appropriate chapters of this book.

Want an overview of the options available?

Then start with **Chapter two**, which looks at the alternative routes available to you, describes them briefly, analyses the advantages and disadvantages of each, then moves on to describe the decisions you need to make and the timing of them.

Keen to find out about starting work at 18?

Then read **Chapter three**, which covers both jobs and Apprenticeships. In fact, since many employers that offer good training and development are using the Apprenticeship system, the distinction between Apprenticeship and job is not actually all that clear cut. You will find a comprehensive list of the different jobs that are usually available to people with level 3 qualifications, so that you can use this chapter to find out about training and employment in particular career areas *or* to get some ideas if you are still at the 'I want a job but I don't know what's on offer' stage. You will also find information on the types of qualification you can work towards once in employment. This chapter also, like several others, contains case studies. The people who feature in them describe what they are doing – and very importantly – how they made their decisions and which sources of advice and information they used to help them to reach them.

Want to find out more about higher education?

Then look at **Chapters four, six** and **seven**.

It is all too easy to simply carry on doing a subject or subjects that you have already done for A level to degree or Higher National Diploma level. Now there is nothing wrong with doing this! If you really love a subject and want to continue it, going even further into depth – great. If you would feel happier doing a subject that you are familiar with – equally fine. But there are literally dozens of subjects that you can start from scratch too. If this idea might appeal then look at **Chapter four**, where you will find a list of suggested new subjects. Higher education has a vocabulary or jargon all of its own, so you will also find in this chapter some definitions of phrases that are commonly used in universities and colleges. There are also case studies of students who describe how their courses are organised, which teaching methods are used and how they manage their time.

People choose courses for different reasons. Everyone's criteria are different. You don't have to follow all the advice and tips in **Chapter six**, but you might find some of the suggested pointers useful. This chapter also contains case studies of students who explain how and why they chose their courses. Some wanted to stick with familiar subjects. Others wanted to try something new. Some had to do a specific course because they wanted to enter a particular career – like medicine. Some students talk about how they chose the places where they are studying. One, for instance, wanted a big city while another wanted a smaller campus institution where she would feel happier, coming as she does from a small place. Another wanted to stay at home and so looked only at a selection of local universities and colleges.

Paying for higher education courses is something that exercises people's minds these days. **Chapter seven** is the chapter for you if you are wondering about how much university might cost. This book was being written just as information about the arrangements for fees and student support from 2006/7 was being made available. So this chapter provides you with a useful introduction to what it all could cost, and to the financial assistance available. Websites and addresses are given, so you can check for further up-to-date information. You will also find case studies of students showing how they manage (or do not manage!) their finances.

Wondering how to find out more?

Whether it is employment or higher education that interests you, or if you haven't yet decided between the two options, you will most probably need some sources of information or need to know who you can ask for advice. Since some of these are common sources they have been put together in **Chapter five**.

Considering taking a gap year?

Then look at **Chapter eight**. A very common option nowadays is to take a gap year or year out. It's often done by students who are going on to university or college but decide to take time out first – but there is no reason why someone who is aiming at an Apprenticeship or job should not have a gap year. Chapter eight gives some ideas on how to fill your gap year.

Need advice on how to make your decision?

Then **Chapter nine** presents you with some questions to help you – and provides some useful guidance on good and bad reasons for choosing a particular route.

Decided on your route but need advice on applying?

Chapter ten deals with applications and interviews for both employment and higher education courses. Again, there are entire books devoted to these matters, so the chapter aims to be concise, giving you the important basic information, while referring you to further sources if you want more detail.

And finally…

a recurring theme throughout this book is that you do not need to make a 'once and for all' decision at this stage, or know exactly what you want to do with your life. The big decision between university/ college or job is not a once and for all decision. You don't cut out all possibility of going on to higher education if you choose the employment option at this stage, as you will see by reading the case studies of Michelle and Tom in Chapter three (pages 42 and 59) – young people who are being sponsored by their employers through a part-time degree course. And many people return to higher education as mature students – see the accounts of Sean, Beth and Michelle in Chapter nine, who have changed track and gone back to learning. In employment too there are opportunities to change: see the case study of Andrew in Chapter three (page 46), who planned two different careers before hitting on the one that is exactly right for him (in the fitness industry). However, the better informed you are, the more likely you are to make the right decisions for yourself from the start, so read on…

Chapter two
Where next?

Once, the basic options for people who had level 3 qualifications were quite simple – work (with or without further training) or more full-time education. Then the idea of taking a gap year before starting higher education became fashionable; hence – option 3. And gap years are not necessarily only for future students; there is no reason why someone leaving education with a level 3 qualification and intending to enter employment should not take a break.

The three options still exist, but they have been joined by another. You could apply to take an Apprenticeship. This option has been around for several years now. Since their introduction, Apprenticeships have encouraged many smaller companies to improve the training they offer to young people.

Work with training

No-one with level 3 qualifications should be thinking about work without training – a dead end job! You may see some such jobs advertised, and the pay might look tempting. But the problem is that the pay wouldn't increase much through your working life, because your prospects of promotion and therefore higher earnings would be severely limited. So please – if employment is a serious consideration, look closely at jobs that have good training built into them. The sorts of jobs that could be open to you ('could' because a lot depends on where you live and on what type of employment is available there) are described in Chapter three. The type of training included in the job could be something relevant to that career only – like a training course in journalism, or it might be a more general qualification that employers like their staff to achieve – like a diploma in science or business studies. You might be given time off during the day to attend a college course that leads to the qualification, or you might be expected to go to evening classes. A third option is to study through distance learning. You might have a choice of study routes. There might be only one available – or there might be different routes but employers choose to use just one of them.

Apprenticeships

These have different titles in the different countries within the United Kingdom – and are explained more fully in Chapter three. An Apprenticeship is a not a recognised stand-alone qualification in its own right (although this may change), but a grouping of qualifications. Apprenticeships enable people to undertake work-based learning that leads to an NVQ level 2 or level 3, demonstrating key skills such as application of number and communication and, in some cases, receiving a technical certificate. The NVQ is awarded for work assessed in the workplace, while the certificate is a qualification that assesses your knowledge and understanding of the job. It is gained through what is known as off-the-job training – which may take place in a college of further education, a specialist training centre for the industry, or at another employer's premises. It may be a qualification that exists already – like a BTEC National Award – or it may be a new one that has been developed especially for the industry that the trainees are working in.

Employers pay their apprentices a wage as an employee, but receive financial assistance from the Government – through different agencies depending on whether you live in England, Northern Ireland, Wales or Scotland. (But you are not likely to be too worried about where the money comes from, as long as you are paid!) What is important for you to know is that in order to receive funding for Apprenticeships, employers have to provide approved training leading to at least an NVQ at the appropriate level. In your case, you should be looking at the level of Apprenticeship that leads to NVQ level 3.

Higher education

You might decide that you want to spend three or more years as a student on a full-time degree or diploma course. This is an increasingly popular option, and the Government is trying to encourage more young people to choose it. You can choose between general or job-related courses, degrees or diplomas; very general courses or very specialised ones; going to a college or a university; and studying at the nearest university or college while living at home or moving to a different town or city and finding accommodation there. Higher education and all the options are described more fully in Chapters four and six.

It does not have to be a full-time option, however. You could study right up to degree level on a part-time basis – and some employers encourage their employees to do exactly that. In this way, you would be combining employment and higher education.

Qualifications

There are so many of these that it can be difficult to find your way through the maze. Do you know the difference between a degree, a Higher National Diploma and a Higher National Certificate? Do you know what postgraduate means? It is also difficult to see how different qualifications relate to or equate to each other. If you look at the charts below things should be made a little clearer. A system of equivalents has been worked out to help you. This has eight levels. (You are already at Point 3).

The National Qualifications Framework

The National Qualifications Framework for England, Wales and Northern Ireland helps students to understand the levels at which qualifications are recognised. The framework detailed below provides a broad indication of how the qualifications compare. You can find out more from the Qualifications and Curriculum Authority (www.qca.org.uk).

Level	Academic	Vocational
8	Doctorate	Specialist award
7	Master's, LLM, MBA	Level 7 Diploma
6	Undergraduate degree Graduate Certificate and Diploma	Level 6 Diploma
5	Diploma of Higher Education Foundation Degree	BTEC Higher National Certificate BTEC Higher National Diploma
4	Certificate of Higher Education	NVQ level 4 (subject to revision)
3	AS and A levels, academic subjects International Baccalaureate	AS and A levels in applied subjects BTEC National Certificate BTEC National Diploma NVQ level 3
2	GCSE (grades A*–C)	GCSEs in vocational subjects (grades A*–C) BTEC First Diploma NVQ level 2 Level 2 Certificate/Diploma
1	GCSE (grades D–G)	GCSEs in vocational subjects (grades D–G) BTEC Introductory Certificate BTEC Introductory Diploma NVQ level 1 Level 1 Certificate/Diploma

The Scottish Credit and Qualifications Framework

Scotland has a different way of setting out the comparisons.

SCQF level	SQA National units, courses and group awards	Higher education	Scottish Vocational Qualifications*
12		Doctorates	
11		Master's	SVQ 5
10		Honours degree Graduate Diploma	
9		Ordinary Degree Graduate Certificate	
8		HND Dip.HE	SVQ 4
7	Advanced Higher	HNC Certificate in higher education	
6	Higher		SVQ 3
5	Intermediate 2 Credit Standard Grade		SVQ 2
4	Intermediate 1 General Standard Grade		SVQ 1
3-1	Access 3-1		

* The positioning of SVQs in the table gives a broad indication of their place within the framework.

Deciding on the right route

You will have appreciated by now that you have a choice to make – and several alternatives. It's *your* choice. A great deal depends on your personality and interests. *You* decide on the right course of action for you. Don't just follow what your friends are doing. You and they are all different. Make your own decision. Try the checklist below and get your answers into focus.

- Has my career choice an entry route at both 18+ and 21+?

- Can I train for the job I want after A levels/BTEC National qualifications etc?

- Is it an all-graduate recruitment career?

- Is there evidence of a preference for 18+ entry in the career area of my choice?

- Have I even made a career choice yet?

- Am I interested in higher education?

- Are there new subjects that attract me?

- Do I want to do a degree in a general subject and decide on a career later?

- Would I find that a waste of time? Must any training I do relate to a career?

- Are there subjects that I previously dropped and would like to take up again?

- Would I be much more suited to learning while earning – i.e. work with training?

- Am I prepared to go to evening classes after a day's work – and do some study during the weekends?

- Is there an Apprenticeship in the career or career area I've chosen?

- What is my attitude to debt (i.e. student loans)?

- Does my financial situation lead me in one direction rather than another?

- Do I know enough about grants, sponsorships, bursaries and scholarships for students in full-time higher education?

Each of the major routes you can choose has a number of advantages and disadvantages.

What are the advantages and disadvantages of employment?

For employment:

- financial independence

- regular pay

- no student debt

- the chance to get straight into training for a job

- no more full-time study

- the chance to work for qualifications that are relevant to a job

- the security of having a job now rather than gambling on getting a better one in three or four years' time.

Against employment:

- it may take longer to qualify in a profession by this route

- people who enter a job at 18 usually earn less over a lifetime than people with higher education qualifications

- you will have to know what kind of job you want to do

- you are likely to be restricted to employment opportunities available in your home area – graduates are usually more mobile because their starting salaries are higher

- you would have to give up some free time to attend evening classes, complete the homework necessary to pass exams and/or obtain qualifications

- study would be after a day's work

- it may not be possible to reach the same level in your job as it would be with a degree

- some jobs cannot be entered without a relevant degree or diploma.

What are the advantages and disadvantages of full-time higher education?

For full-time higher education:

- time to enjoy yourself and spread your wings without having the pressure of having to learn a job

- the chance to leave home for a relatively structured environment

- the opportunity to make friends from different areas and backgrounds – many of whom you'll keep for life

- the possibility of keeping your options open – you don't have to decide on a career yet

- or – if you do know what career you want and will choose a vocational degree or diploma – you'll have more time to do your academic work

- in other words – more free time.

Against full-time higher education:

- not seeing any relevance in what you study

- you might still have to do lengthy training when you leave university

- having to leave home, whether you want to do so or not, if the course is not available locally

- losing several years' earnings

- missing out on work experience

- student debt!

No-one can say accurately how much your higher education might cost if you choose to do it on a full-time basis – or how much you might end up owing when you graduate. When this book was being written the Government estimated that students would leave higher education owing about £15,000, while admitting that any who deferred payment of tuition fees and took out the full student loan could owe more than £22,000 on graduation. This means that they could be still repaying the loans well into their thirties.

If these sorts of figures alarm you, you might like to look more seriously at the possibility of gaining qualifications – and you can get these right up to degree level – while in employment. *But* you also need to weigh up all the factors already mentioned (such as not having a completely free choice of subject to study). You also need to be aware that not all students will have the same level of expenses. There are grants, for instance, to help those from lower income families. So, before you hit instant panic and throw away the university prospectuses, have a look at Chapter seven, which goes into financing higher education in more detail.

Lifelong learning

Whatever you choose to do immediately, you will also certainly have to work for more qualifications at some point(s) during your career. Jobs are changing so rapidly, and the skills needed to do them becoming outdated as a result, so many people, even those working at quite a senior level, are required to update. Indeed, in some professions Continuing Professional Development (CPD) is compulsory if people wish to continue in their jobs. The knowledge and skills you acquire at 18 or 21 will not be relevant for ever.

You might have to:

- attend short courses and conferences provided by your employer

- take part-time courses in the evening

- study through distance learning

- or even retrain completely for a new career.

Some of this training might be provided free of charge. Some might be your own responsibility.

If you are in year 12 (or the equivalent in Scotland)

It's not too early to start thinking about your future. Why? Because if you are going to apply for a higher education course – i.e. at a university or college of higher education, you will be filling in the application forms *one year from now*. You apply a whole year in advance.

If you will be choosing employment instead, you'll need to start applying for jobs a little later – but still well before the end of year 13. (From January onwards.)

If you are already in year 13 (or the equivalent in Scotland)

You will apply for most degree and diploma courses through the Universities and Colleges Admissions Service (UCAS). You do so on one application – which permits you to choose just six courses – and which is returned to UCAS to be recorded and sent to the universities or colleges you have chosen. UCAS has a closing date in January (or October for a small number of courses – such as medicine, veterinary science and any course at Oxford or Cambridge). This is all explained in Chapter ten.

Might you want to take a gap year?

Start looking into possibilities now – especially if you want to do voluntary work overseas. The best schemes recruit early – often by the end of January.

Or you might be considering:

■ earning money to help finance your higher education course

■ getting some relevant experience

■ travelling.

There are several books written for gap-year students that are full of ideas. Check whether there are any in your school/college.

Have you already decided on the employment option?

Don't sit back while all the UCAS applicants are getting on with their applications. Some employers, in particular large national companies, begin to recruit from January.

Before you can apply for any jobs you will need to do the following:

- Prepare a CV or make sure that your Record of Achievement/ Progress File is up to date.

- Make sure that you know how to write a good letter of application, and know what sort of questions to expect on application forms.

- Read about job interview technique – and get a practice interview if you can.

Calendars

Year 12 (or the equivalent in Scotland)

September–December

Start to look at all the options that will be available at the end of year 13.

Choose your A2 subjects with the type of job or course that you are hoping for in mind.

January–March

Start some research into higher education courses and/or jobs and local employment opportunities.

Attend any higher education fairs that are held.

April–July

Attend any higher education fairs that are held.

Start research on individual universities and colleges.

Get prospectuses.

Check entry requirements to courses.

Start to make a list of higher education institutions that might interest you.

Go to some university or college open days.

Arrange work experience or visits to find out more about careers you are interested in.

If you will be applying for a degree course in any career in the medical field, teaching and many other vocational courses, work experience or visits are very important – try to arrange some.

If you will be taking a gap year start researching opportunities – many good schemes fill up very quickly.

If you are interested in sponsorship from an employer or organisation start researching them.

Start to make a list of points to go on your CV or in your higher education personal statement.

Find out about sources of financial support for higher education courses.

Check closing dates for higher education applications – and for any tests that you might have to take.

If you will be applying for an art or design course start to prepare a portfolio.

Year 13 (or the equivalent in Scotland)
September–December

Finalise your higher education choices.

Start work on your UCAS* form. It has to be in by 15 January.

If you are applying to Oxford or Cambridge, or to any university for medicine, dentistry or veterinary science the closing date is 15 October.

If you are applying for a *diploma* course in nursing you must apply to NMAS* by 15 December. (Degree courses are in UCAS.)

If you are applying for art and design courses through Route A* the closing date is the same as for other UCAS applications. For Route B* courses you need to apply next term. Finalise your portfolio.

Apply for any course at a college that is not in a central applications system – such as an art foundation course.

Make sponsorship applications.

Make applications for any appropriate bursaries or scholarships.

Research job opportunities.

Attend any careers conventions or job fairs that are held.

January–April

Send Route B art and design applications by the beginning of March. (The deadline is 24 March but earlier application is advised.)

Apply for financial assistance for higher education.

Start to apply for jobs.

If you do not receive any UCAS offers consider using UCAS EXTRA* from the middle of March.

May–July

Reply to UCAS offers.

Continue to apply for jobs.

Look into part-time higher education opportunities if there are some that will be appropriate to your job.

If you need any help in August following publication of the exam results, contact your Connexions or careers service.

* All these terms are explained in Chapter ten

Chapter three
Work

What's available?

Probably more than you imagine!

As more and more young people head for full-time higher education many employers have become accustomed to recruiting graduates. (Whether they do so because their jobs genuinely require degree level entrants or simply because graduates are around in greater numbers is a point that could be discussed for a long time.) But did you know that some employers still have their own training schemes for people with level 3 qualifications? Some are large companies that may have only one site, so availability of jobs will vary according to where you live. However, other employers of the type that can be found in most areas, such as the National Health Service and local authorities, also recruit 18-year-olds as do the finance sector (accountancy, banking and insurance). Hospitality, leisure and tourism are also worth looking into.

Much will depend, though, on where you live. If you live right in the middle of a large city you won't find a traineeship in forestry too easy to come by. If you live in a small village in the middle of a National Park, you would have to travel a long way to find work in engineering. Obvious? Yes. But what isn't always so obvious is that you can train for a range of different jobs with just one employer. Say you had thought about becoming an accountant. You might start looking through the *Yellow Pages* for the addresses of accountancy firms. But would you have thought of the big chocolate factory which employs a lot of people? It will have an accounts department and may well recruit trainee accounting technicians or accountants. It might also train school and college leavers in its IT, customer service, company secretarial, personnel, legal and marketing departments. It might be possible to find a job as an administrative assistant in any of the departments, and work for NVQs or follow an Apprenticeship in Management Support.

Large companies, however, are not the sole providers of work with good training and prospects. As pointed out earlier, the introduction of Apprenticeships has enabled many smaller employers who do not have the luxury of large training and human resources departments to offer better training to their workforce. You could find a job with a very small organisation – which uses the resources of an outside training consultancy to help plan its training.

All this means that you need to discover just what is available locally in general terms – and then watch for situations vacant like a hawk. Don't try to do this all on your own. Enlist help. It's particularly important to do this if you have, as yet, no clear idea about the type of career you want. Arrange to see a careers adviser or personal adviser (careers) as they are sometimes known. Hopefully, you already know one because they visit your school or college. If not, look the organisation up in the phone book and ask how to make an appointment.

Careers information and advice are provided by local offices of:

■ the Connexions service, in England

■ the Careers service, Northern Ireland

■ Careers Scotland

■ Careers Wales.

Careers Scotland and Careers Wales, incidentally, have very useful websites. English students can find a lot of useful information on the Connexions website – and might also find that a local website is provided by their Connexions Partnership.

Jobs

The jobs that are most commonly available to people with level 3 qualifications are summarised in the following lists. There is a warning, however. The fact that a job appears in the list doesn't mean that you will automatically be able to find one at 17/18 plus. For the reasons already discussed they might just not be available in your area, or the career area might well be available but employers have a policy of recruiting students leaving higher education. Some of the jobs are more usually entered by university and college leavers. Others you might not be able to enter straightaway, but could do if you did an Apprenticeship or gained suitable experience in the career first, and then qualified further when you had started work. For example, it would be unlikely that your local authority would employ you as trainee housing manager, but it might take you on as an assistant in a housing department and provide you with further training if you seemed keen. But if a job does not have a degree or level 4 Diploma as a minimum entry requirement, it's on the list!

To help you locate jobs more easily they are divided into groups.

For people who are taking science subjects

It is important to check which of the different science subjects – biology, chemistry, physics or general science will be required for individual jobs.

- agricultural worker/management trainee
- arboricultural management trainee
- assistant scientific officer, Civil Service
- complementary medicine practitioner (some jobs)
- conservation assistant/officer, museums
- critical care technologist
- engineering technician/technologist
- fish farm worker/management trainee
- food science technician/technologist
- forestry worker/management trainee
- horticultural worker/management trainee
- laboratory/scientific technician/technologist
- Merchant Navy engineering officer
- nutritional therapist
- quality controller
- veterinary nurse.

If you qualify for the jobs in the science group, you can also consider the following list.

Jobs for people taking humanities or social science subjects (and who have GCSE/S grades that include maths and physical or double integrated science at A-C/1-3)

- air traffic controller
- architectural technician/technologist
- Army technician
- computer business analyst
- computer hardware technician
- computer programmer
- construction manager
- construction/building technician
- consumer adviser
- countryside ranger
- crime scene examiner
- database operator
- dispensing optician
- IT operator
- medical photographer
- Merchant Navy deck officer*
- operating department practitioner
- pharmacy technician
- pilot, civil aviation
- Royal Air Force technician

* A levels/Highers in maths and physics gives entry to an accelerated training scheme with some companies.

- Royal Navy technician
- systems analyst
- website developer.

If you qualify for these jobs you can also look at the following list.

Jobs for people studying humanities or social science subjects (and who have maths at GCSE/S grade A-C/1-3)

- accountant
- accounting technician
- actuary*
- Army officer
- auctioneer
- bank officer/manager
- building society worker
- building surveyor
- bursar
- buyer/purchasing officer
- cartographic technician
- chartered surveyor (building control, general practice, insurance, land, property, quantity, rural practice)
- civil engineering technician
- computer operator/programmer
- Diplomatic Service officer
- engineering construction technician
- financial services adviser

* Maths at A level or Higher grade is required

- freight forwarder
- health service administrator
- heating, refrigeration and air conditioning technician
- housing manager
- importer/exporter
- market researcher
- prison officer
- quantity surveyor
- Royal Air Force officer
- Royal Navy/Royal Marines officer
- stock exchange worker
- surveyor, general practice
- tax consultant
- technical surveyor
- transport manager

And you can also look at the following list.

Jobs for people studying humanities or social science subjects (and who have no maths or science GCSE/S grades A-C/1-3)

But, be warned that many individual employers will still ask for a maths pass.

- administrator
- advertising account executive
- advertising media executive
- air cabin crew

- airline/airport administrator
- ambulance technician/paramedic
- Armed Forces (non-commissioned)
- Civil Service, junior manager/administrative officer
- commercial administrator
- court administrative officer
- court reporter
- Revenue and Customs officer
- distribution manager
- estate agent
- fast food outlet manager
- firefighter
- health and safety officer
- human resources (personnel) manager
- immigration officer
- insurance broker
- insurance claims assessor
- insurance claims settler
- insurance technician
- insurance underwriter
- journalist
- legal executive
- leisure centre manager
- library assistant
- licensed conveyancer

- local government administrator
- loss adjuster
- market researcher
- marketing executive/assistant
- photographer
- planner
- planning technician
- Police officer
- public relations officer
- recruitment agency consultant
- residential social worker
- retail manager
- sales executive
- secretary
- tourist information centre assistant
- travel agent.

The European dimension

You now have the right to work in any country that is part of the European Union (EU) either temporarily (perhaps to get some work experience or to learn a language) or permanently. You would have more chance of getting a job in another country, though, if you first had relevant skills and qualifications – and some work experience behind you. If you do decide that you would like to work abroad at some stage you can contact the following sources for information and advice:

- your local Jobcentre Plus – they have access to European vacancies (ask about the EURES vacancy network)

- UK or multinational companies that have links in other countries or who operate across Europe

- the European institutions (European Commission, European Parliament etc) – the Commission offers some work experience or stagiare placements

- your local Connexions or careers centre.

(The EU member states are Austria, Belgium, Cyprus, Czech Republic, Denmark, Estonia, Finland, France, Germany, Greece, Hungary, Ireland, Italy, Latvia, Lithuania, Luxembourg, Malta, Poland, Portugal, Slovakia, Slovenia, Spain, Sweden, The Netherlands and The United Kingdom.)

Apprenticeships

Apprenticeships are for people who have left full-time education. You probably heard about them in careers lessons in year 11. They consist of work experience and training for a job, and they give young people specific skills that employers want. Employers are heavily involved in drawing up the programmes. At their request, Apprenticeship programmes also include a number of key skills:

- application of number

- communication

- improving your learning and performance

- information technology

- problem solving

- working with others.

There are over 100 different Apprenticeships (for example, in animal care, cultural heritage, health and beauty therapy, tourism…), although they might not all be available where you live – and not all are available at the Higher level.

How do they work?

Advanced Apprenticeships (England) and *Modern* Apprenticeships (Scotland and Wales) are intended for people who have the ability to gain high-level skills and qualifications, and can lead to a full-time job and the option of carrying on to HND, HNC or degree level. They last at least 24 months, but can take three or four years to complete. On one of these programmes you would be aiming for supervisory, technical or junior management level work, and training to NVQ/SVQ level 3 – sometimes 4. Yes – you would be gaining a second level 3 qualification if you chose this route – but this one would be in a career-related area. You might also gain a professional qualification. For example, a young person doing an Apprenticeship in the equine industry could be working towards an NVQ/SVQ and also take the examinations of the British Horse Society in riding instruction or stable management. It is also possible to be studying for the qualification of the Association of Accounting Technicians (AAT) while on an Apprenticeship. With the AAT qualification it is possible to progress to chartered accountancy training.

Advanced and Modern Apprentices are employees and are paid an appropriate wage. If you opt for this kind of training an employer will put together a training programme so that you can see exactly what you are entitled to expect – and which has to be agreed by you both. This programme will be unique to you and will include some off-the-job training that you might receive at your place of work if your employer is approved to give it. If not, you might attend college on day or block release, the training centre of another employer in the same sector, or a training centre for the industry. Most small businesses use an external college or training provider to provide the off-the-job learning part of the Apprenticeship. Apprentices in travel agencies for instance – which are often small businesses and might have only one apprentice – sometimes attend courses that are run by a specialist travel training provider, together with Apprentices from other agencies. Employers are advised on suitable training providers in the area by the local office of the national organisation that oversees Apprenticeships (for example, the Learning and Skills Council for England).

Many Advanced Apprentices now continue their education and training by enrolling on foundation degree courses. In some areas there are close links, which mean that people move from the Apprenticeship to the degree programme almost as a matter of course. For example there is a scheme – a Higher Apprenticeship in IT, which leads from an Apprenticeship to a foundation degree and from there to a full honours degree if wished. Job openings could include computer business analyst, computer hardware technician, computer programmer, IT operator, systems analyst and website developer.

At present you would do your entire Apprenticeship with one employer. However, the Learning and Skills Council is looking at the possibility of offering greater flexibility, so that an apprentice can take a part-completed Apprenticeship with them if they move to a different employer.

There may be more than one Apprenticeship available in the type of work you are looking for – just as more than one company may be taking trainees in the same line of work. You do not have to apply for one only.

Facts and figures

■ During the academic year 2004/05, 28% of 16- to 21-year-olds entered Apprenticeships – over 176,000 young people.

■ And a second target that all 16- and 17-year-olds with five or more GCSE passes should be entitled to an Apprenticeship place.

■ There are now more than 255,000 young people currently training in 180 different Apprenticeships.

■ Over 50% of apprentices are training in five main sectors – business administration, construction, engineering, manufacturing and retail.

■ Employers using Apprenticeships range from very small businesses to very large ones like Asda, BMW, British Gas and Tesco.

To summarise

At the end of an Apprenticeship you would have received:

■ practical experience, skills and knowledge

■ an NVQ/SVQ at at least level 3 for an Advanced/Modern Apprenticeship

■ key skills qualifications (for instance in working in teams, solving problems, communication, and use of new technology)

■ a technical certificate like a BTEC National Diploma or City & Guilds Progression Award

■ additional qualifications that are necessary or useful in your particular job.

More lists

The full list of Apprenticeships on offer (in England) as this book was being written was as follows.

■ accounting

■ active leisure and learning

■ advice and guidance

■ agriculture and garden machinery

■ agriculture, crops and livestock

■ amenity horticulture

■ animal care

■ arts and entertainment

■ aviation

■ bakery

■ beauty therapy

■ broadcast, film, video and multimedia

■ building services engineers

- business administration
- call handling
- ceramics
- chemical, pharmaceutical, petrochemical manufacturing and refining industries
- cleaning and support services
- clothing industry
- community justice
- construction
- cultural heritage
- customer service
- driving goods vehicles
- early years care and education
- electrical and electronic servicing
- electricity industry
- electrotechnical
- emergency fire services operations
- engineering
- environmental conservation
- equine industry
- events
- farriery
- fence installation industry
- fibreboard packaging
- floristry
- food and drink manufacturing
- furniture manufacturing

- gas industry
- glass industry
- hairdressing
- health and social care
- heating, ventilating, air conditioning and refrigeration
- hospitality
- housing
- industrial applications
- information and library services
- information technology and electronic services
- insurance
- international trade services
- jewellery, silversmithing and allied trades
- laboratory technicians
- land passenger transport: maintaining automotive vehicles
- land-based service engineering
- learning and development/direct training and support
- management
- man-made fibres
- manufacturing
- marine industry
- meat and poultry processing
- mechanical engineering services: plumbing
- motor industry
- newspapers
- occupational health and safety

- oil and gas extraction

- operating department practice

- optical manufacturing technician

- paper and board manufacture

- payroll

- personnel

- pharmacy technicians

- photo-imaging

- physiological measurement technology

- polymer processing

- ports industry

- print and print packaging

- procurement

- production horticulture

- providing financial services

- rail engineering

- rail operations

- residential estate agency and residential property letting and management agency

- retailing

- road haulage and distribution

- sales and telesales

- sea-fishing

- security systems

- sign-making
- steel and metals industry
- surface coatings industry
- telecommunications
- textiles
- timber industry
- travel services
- water industry
- wholesale, distribution, warehousing and storage.

Most popular Advanced Apprenticeships

In descending order, the top ten (in England) are:

	Numbers in training
engineering	17,147
automotive industry	13,623
electrotechnical	11,650
early years care and education	7169
hospitality	4958
business administration	4651
customer service	4406
construction	3901
health and social care	3775
hairdressing	3095

The numbers are for Advanced apprentices in training when last counted – in April 2005.

Some Apprentices

Paul

Retail store manager

Paul started his training with an Advanced Apprenticeship in customer service and began his training with a role working in a stock room, but he had the ambition to attain management level and progressed to an Advanced Apprenticeship in management. He was soon promoted to stock manager and then, after only six months in that role, to sales manager. He feels that it was with the help of the Apprenticeship programme that he developed the skills to be a successful manager. This was confirmed when he won the Sales Manager of the Year Award for the Midlands Area. Now a store manager, he enjoys implementing new ideas and increasing staff morale, productivity and profit. One of his ideas has been to introduce a 'manager's special promotion' which contributed £50,000 in extra sales over 30 weeks; another was to instigate flexible opening hours over the Christmas period, generating £22,000 worth of extra sales. He has also test-run an internet-based training programme for his staff, which has improved their skills and resulted in the store being in the top three in the area for 'mystery shopper' audits.

Paul was the regional Advanced Apprentice of the Year, in 2004.

Michelle

Advanced Apprentice (engineering), with an aerospace company

Michelle has A levels in geography, psychology, art and general studies. As she says, they are not subjects that would lead automatically to a career in engineering, but at the time she chose her subjects she wanted to be a graphic designer.

'I had enjoyed graphic design very much for GCSE but it wasn't offered as an A level, so I chose art instead.

However, I found art too abstract. I enjoyed the applied side and the technical drawing aspect. I didn't enjoy the emphasis on creative work. I decided to apply to university to study applied engineering product design – and was offered places. But I was influenced by a friend two years ahead of me who was doing an engineering apprenticeship at this company and decided to apply to the company at the same time as I did my UCAS application. I was accepted to do an Advanced Apprenticeship in engineering, with the promise that if I completed the Apprenticeship successfully, the company would send me to university to do a part-time degree course.

It was a four-year Apprenticeship with the first year spent in gaining hands-on experience. That year was not related either to design engineering or to aircraft. All the Apprentices gained experience in the company's training school, working on machinery, toolmaking and electrical installations. Then we spent six months working on the shop floor – on aircraft. After that came four months' experience in each of five different areas, and we could then choose to specialise in one for six months. I chose design engineering at this point and worked with computer-aided-design packages to create 3D models and 2D drawings of aircraft.

During the first year I had day release to college to study for a National Certificate in mechanical and electrical engineering. In the second year the day release continued but we had to spend one evening at college as well. I gained the qualifications successfully and moved on to a Higher National Certificate. I converted this into a Higher National Diploma just after I completed the Apprenticeship. In the workplace I gained NVQ level 2 in engineering and level 3 in aerospace engineering. I also had to do key skills. Numeracy and IT were not a problem but I did find the units in communication rather challenging at first. (We had exams for this which involved summarising articles and picking out the main points.) I had to keep portfolios of evidence, showing tasks I had completed and skills I had gained for both the NVQs and for the key skills.

I'm about to start my degree course in mechanical engineering which will take one day and evening a week at Blackburn College and will lead to a degree from Lancaster University. My employers will pay all the fees and continue to pay my full salary while I'm studying.

I consider that I have the best of both worlds. I'm going to end up with a degree just as though I had gone to uni full time, but I have been paid a salary all the time and have gained a lot of additional practical and key skills and valuable work experience. I want to progress to at least team leader level here, although I'm not yet sure about aiming for a senior management job. I know about the training route for graduates which leads to chartered engineer status and I will probably decide to do that when I have my degree.'

Danielle

Advanced Apprentice/trainee accounting technician

Danielle, who has AS levels in business studies, economics and psychology, is just about to start her last year of training.

'I considered university during my A level course – but I was only interested in finding a specifically vocational course. I didn't want to study a subject that wasn't going to qualify me for anything. I also wanted to stay at home and live with my parents. This meant that my choice of universities was very limited. My A levels seemed to lead me in the direction of accountancy, so I asked my careers teacher about training. She told me that I could do it through a degree course or in employment and gave me some basic information.

I then made an appointment to see my personal adviser from Connexions who I had discussed options with previously at the end of my AS year. We had talked about financial work then. She confirmed that I had a choice of routes to follow and should be able to get a job quite easily if that was what I wanted, but she did stress that I should look for one that would offer me good training. She suggested that I look into AAT training (leading to the qualification of the Association of Accounting Technicians). I went along to my local college to find out about full-time courses first. However, I was told that I could also do the course there on a part-time basis and that the college could find an employer who would sponsor me. This was absolutely perfect! I started as an Advanced Apprentice with a firm that they found for me.

It didn't quite work out though – but I was able to change employer while continuing the Apprenticeship. I now work for a large firm of structural engineers and get block-release to college. It works out at four days each month. I'm doing the course with people who work in different companies but they are not all doing the training through an Apprenticeship. I think the Apprenticeship route is good because the training that I should be getting at work is specified, and an assessor comes in regularly to see me and also to talk to my boss and make sure that my college work and job-based training tie in with each other.

I work in the accounts office with ten other people – but I am the only Apprentice there. I started off doing quite routine work, like checking invoices, but I have been promoted recently to finance co-ordinator and now help the professional accountants to produce the monthly and annual sets of management accounts.

I am just starting the third year of AAT training and will have to decide at the end of it whether I want to continue training and become an accountant. My tutor at college has suggested that I should, but I can have a very satisfying job as an accounts technician – so I haven't made my mind up about this yet. If I do decide to continue I'll be able to qualify as either a certified or management accountant by working for the exams of either the Association of Chartered Certified Accountants or the Chartered Institute of Management Accountants.

I'm so glad that I chose this route. I shall soon have a recognised qualification and have no student debts to pay off.'

Andrew

Assistant gym manager, training through an Advanced Apprenticeship

Andrew, who has A levels in art and design and photography, has reached his present position through on-the-job training with a fitness company. He is now taking advanced qualifications which should help him in his future career with the assistance of an Advanced Apprenticeship programme.

'It has taken me a while to work out what I finally want to do with my life! I left school at 16 and spent two years in retailing, eventually working my way up to the position of assistant manager. At this point I decided that I might regret later the fact that I had finished my education so early. So I went to college full-time to do A levels. I chose the subjects with a view to doing further training in photography.

I applied for degree courses and went for interviews at different universities and colleges. I then began to have serious doubts. I was two years older than many students. I would leave with debts of about £15,000 – and I had no guarantee that I would get a job in photography. I realised that I didn't want to commit three years to uncertain prospects. So – I began to look around for a job.

I was a member of a leisure centre and did regular workouts there. I decided to see if there were any trainee positions available. There was nothing on the gym side but there were vacancies for lifeguards. I decided to apply for one of those positions as a way of getting my foot in the door. I was offered a job – but in the meantime I had been to talk to the fitness centre manager who told me that he would soon be recruiting for some trainees to do a company-sponsored training course. I applied and was successful.

The training provided was a really good deal. Qualifications in the leisure industry can be very expensive to obtain. The company that ran the fitness centre put me through an intensive two-week course to obtain the YMCA level 2 qualification in gym instructing (which is widely respected in the industry). The deal was that if I left the job in less than 12 months I would have to repay the cost of the course. However, I didn't do so. I was enjoying the work too much! As a fitness instructor I worked directly with customers, working out exercise programmes for them, showing them how to use the equipment and motivating them to continue.

I had been promoted to assistant gym manager and was wondering how I was going to manage to afford to get higher qualifications when I suddenly received a call from someone in marketing at a local training provider. I was told all about Advanced Apprenticeships and informed that I could apply to do one without changing job or taking a cut in salary. It seemed too good to be true!

I took up the offer – and I am getting excellent training free of charge! I am doing all the work in my own time – but as assistant manager I draw up the staffing rotas and have been able to organise it so that I and some other people who are working for qualifications can work suitable shifts. When I finish the Apprenticeship I shall have both the YMCA level 3 in professional gym instructing and NVQ level 3 in instructing exercise and fitness. I have completed the YMCA part and have just to finish off my folder of evidence for the NVQ.

I have had absolutely all the training that I need for the future without having to get into debt – or indeed have to pay anything at all. I have also been able to train in a hands-on environment which for me is much more suitable than a full-time course would have been.

My immediate ambition is to become the youngest gym manager in the company – which I think I'm on target to achieve. Ultimately, I would like to have by own business as a personal trainer and convert space in my house to use as a gym. In the meantime I am getting experience by doing personal training sessions with friends and some members of my family.'

What's in it for employers?

The Government hasn't introduced Apprenticeships just for the good of *your* health. There has to be something in it for industry otherwise employers wouldn't cooperate. The good ones would continue to use their own training programmes, and the bad ones would continue to do nothing much. As you have read, employers get financial incentives to take apprentices. They also get help and advice on suitable training providers (if they need to use them) from local representatives of the agencies that run the Apprenticeship programmes. A third major benefit to them is that they get keen, motivated people who are willing to invest in their own training by working for NVQs and other qualifications. (There is currently a skills gap in the UK. That's bad for the nation's competitiveness at a global level.)

This is what a selection of employers say.

Dukeries

Dukeries in Mansfield, Nottinghamshire, is a medium-sized building company that employs 120 people. Every year it recruits and trains a number of apprentices. The advantages to the company are summed up by Glenn Manners, the managing director, as being a better trained workforce for the company – and also employees who develop a loyalty to the firm and want to stay there. 'Dukeries attributes the success and professionalism of the company largely to the success of Apprenticeships. The benefits of Apprenticeships training are numerous. We're committed in full to the development of youngsters in partnership with their parents, coaches and mentors. By clearly demonstrating our pleasure in their successes, we've generated commitment and loyalty that doesn't just come from the apprentices but from all the partners involved. The bottom line is that Apprenticeships have helped our business at all levels; the obvious effect on our morale and retention has been phenomenal. Of all the apprentices who have completed their training only one has not remained with Dukeries. Several have indicated their desire to continue their development here, and indeed one of them is now training as health and safety assistant with an ambition to become the company's health and safety officer in a few years.

Apprentices keep our company young and vibrant in our corporate outlook and our clients love it. We could not now imagine our company without them.'

BAe Systems

BAe Systems is an international company that engages in the development, delivery and support of advanced defence aerospace systems. The company employs more than 90,000 people and generates sales of over £12 billion, and needs staff with expert design and manufacturing know-how available 24 hours a day, seven days a week. It also needs trained people to introduce products and to provide customer service. To meet these requirements, BAE Systems typically recruits around 280 apprentices a year.

John Lee Male, head of learning and development at BAe Systems says that the Advanced Apprenticeship programme attracts new people to the industry and enables young people without any engineering or business experience to develop their skills. It also allows BAE Systems to tackle the national shortage of qualified engineering staff. In addition 'The low attrition rate of the programme ensures that BAe Systems maintains and enhances its staff capability with enthusiastic and capable young people who often fill senior positions as their careers develop. Apprentices provide BAe Systems with a higher net return on investment than externally recruited employees, and due to shorter training periods after qualification provide a good resource pool for further enhancement of skills. Apprentices who start their working life with the company have high retention rates as a result (87%). Attracting, training and retaining high quality apprentices helps BAe Systems keep its competitive edge. Our apprentices are self motivated, ready to take the initiative and go into problem solving mode, therefore reducing production time for the work they do by up to 25%.'

Tesco

Clare Chapman, group human resources director for Tesco, says 'Giving our people the skills they need to do their jobs is key to our success. Our Apprenticeship pilot is already getting great feedback from staff, who tell us they like the opportunity to earn and learn, and is part of our continued commitment to giving our staff the opportunity to get on. We are keen to continue building on our already successful training programmes. Early signs from the pilot are encouraging, with staff getting real benefits from the scheme. Tesco is a learning organisation and wants to ensure its people have an opportunity to get on, which is why we continue to invest heavily in training and development for our staff, giving them the tools to do their job.'

Training

Whether you train with an employer through their own training scheme or through an Apprenticeship there are different ways of learning and qualifying. Training divides into two different but closely related parts, practical and theoretical. The first is given at work and might be carried out in one department or involve you in gaining experience in several. The second could be done through block release, day release, evening classes or distance learning. Definitions of these terms are given on page 70.

Qualifications

As part of your training you might be required to enrol for a part-time foundation degree, part-time honours degree or Higher National level qualification. These are all higher education qualifications and are described fully in Chapter four. Alternatively, your employer might prefer you to study for a qualification that is organised especially for the kind of job you are doing.

Professional/vocational qualifications

Some common examples are those offered by the following organisations.

- The Association of Accounting Technicians

- The Institutes of Chartered, Certified, Management and Public Finance Accountancy

- The Association of British Dispensing Opticians

- The British Horse Society

- The National Council for the Training of Journalists (NCTJ)

- The Institute of Legal Executives

- The Institute of Leisure and Amenity Management.

NCTJ trainees, for example, follow a prescribed pattern of training whichever newspaper they are working for and take the same exams. (Non NCTJ trainees may follow a training programme drawn up by their newspaper group.)

These are just some examples of professional qualifications.

National Vocational Qualifications (NVQs)

These are job-related qualifications that have been designed in close cooperation with employers. They are designed to help you show what you can *do* rather than the exams you can pass. You would gain NVQs by successfully learning skills and achieving tasks in your place of work. An NVQ assessor would sign a statement that you would keep, to confirm that you had successfully completed each one. This would go in a log or training diary that you would keep in a portfolio of evidence to show what you had achieved. The assessor could be someone where you worked, who had taken special training, or could be someone from outside.

There are five levels. Level 3 is equivalent to A levels and National Diplomas. Levels 4 and 5 are at higher education level. You can gain NVQs on an Apprenticeship programme, or in a job. They are open to everyone at any stage of their careers. There is no age cut-off point.

Training leading to NVQs is often offered in a limited range of jobs, where neither Apprenticeships nor professional qualifications are available. Your employer may offer this automatically – or you might have to ask. What you can do is ask your careers or Connexions adviser exactly what is available in the career area, before approaching your employer with the request to be supported to undertake the training.

Supported? Yes. Training costs money and if your employer is willing to pay for tuition fees, textbooks and examination entry fees this will be less to come out of your pocket. Good employers are usually willing to give day release to employees to allow them to attend college courses. If they don't – it doesn't necessarily follow that they are bad employers! There may not be any appropriate courses. There may be some but not held on a day that suits the business. The business may be too small to permit anyone to be absent (in which case it would help if you were willing to attend evening classes). Of course, on a scheme such as an Apprenticeship training is included, and you don't have to pay for it.

Scottish Vocational Qualifications

Scottish Vocational Qualifications (SVQs) are the Scottish parallel qualifications to the English NVQs. SVQs are available for a wide range of occupational areas, at five levels.

Some people in jobs and how they are training

Distance learning and block release

Not all further study involves attending regular classes. Many people taking qualifications while working learn through distance learning (or you may be familiar with the more traditional term correspondence courses). This involves self-study at home, sending assignments to be marked to the organisation. Tutor back-up may be provided through such means as email, the telephone etc. Some distance learning courses involve attending occasional residential weekends or weeks. The case study below illustrates an example of this way of learning.

Geeta

Trainee dispensing optician with a large national chain

'I did science A levels – maths and physics – because I had no idea about a career and at my careers interview in year 11 my personal adviser suggested that the best thing would be to take these subjects as I was good at them. He said that they led to a really big range of careers.

I had a weekend job all through year 12 in an outdoor shop, and discovered that I really enjoyed advising customers when they came to buy equipment. (I am heavily into climbing and mountain walking.) So when I came to think about choosing a university course I started to think about something in the medical field – perhaps radiography or physiotherapy where I could help and advise people. I also discovered that I would have my tuition fees paid by the NHS and might also get a bursary. Some work experience put me off though. There was too much physical contact with sick people to be honest. I then thought about sports science, but when I weighed up the cost of a three-year degree course without the NHS money I decided 'No way'.

I looked in a book in my school library, which was about getting a job after A levels, to see what I could do – and I found just the right job. The girl in the book talked about her training in optician work, and I liked the bit where she talked about spending a lot of time finding out what customers needed for their lifestyle and then helping them to choose glasses that suited their appearance too.

The training is brilliant. I'm learning a lot of the practical stuff at work, mainly from the manager who is in charge of my training, but from other qualified opticians too. I don't go to evening classes or anything for the theory. I do that at home in my spare time. I have to do a lot of reading on physics, anatomy and optics, and complete question papers almost every two weeks. All the stuff is sent to me at home, so I have no excuse for forgetting to do it. It does take eight to ten hours every week – which is a drawback, but I think it's worth it not to have to pay off a huge loan at the end of a full-time course. Because I'm busy climbing most weekends, I try to be disciplined and work for three hours on three evenings during the week. Later this year the company will send me down to London for a four-week residential theory course, and will pay all my expenses.'

In-house training

Other employers run their own training programmes, which do not lead to any external qualifications. If you joined the Civil Service, Police or Armed Forces or went into retailing, your training would be almost entirely on the job although you might be sent on short courses from time to time.

Matt

Trainee hotel manager with a national group

'I didn't know what I wanted to do after taking an AVCE in business*. I didn't want anything that seemed too 'businessy'

* now applied business A level

and certainly not heavily financial. If anything, the AVCE showed me what I didn't want to do rather than giving me ideas on what I would like! So I took a summer job in a theme park – just as a way of earning some money and giving myself time to think. While I was there I realised that I enjoyed working with people and decided to find out about possibilities of jobs in this line.

I went to see a careers adviser who asked me all sorts of questions about myself and about my aspirations, whether I wanted a full-time course or whether if I went into a job with training I would mind going to college in the evenings. I also completed a computer questionnaire which suggested a list of jobs. Most of them I ruled out straightaway. There were one or two – like social worker and paramedic – that I did look into further, but I decided against them. I didn't want quite that amount of close involvement with other people. Law came up high on the list too, but I decided against that because of all the study involved. I told the adviser that I knew my limitations pretty well when it came to study, and that I had basically had enough! We then began to talk about the service sector. I liked the idea of retailing to begin with, because she explained that I could get to be the manager of my own shop quite quickly on merit rather than qualifications. Then she mentioned the hospitality industry, and I was very keen to find out more. I'd helped out from time to time in the bars and restaurants at the theme park and it seemed OK. She stressed that I shouldn't go back to a dead-end job with no prospects and I thought 'Yeah, Yeah. We've been here.'

The outcome was that she put me in touch with a hotel chain that did take trainees and treat them properly. I applied, was interviewed – and I'm here. The training period usually takes 18 months before you get your first assistant manager job in a small hotel, and I am on target to achieve that.

My training is exactly as I wanted. I have worked in every department – administration, front desk, kitchens, housekeeping, guest services, leisure centre, conference and events – you name it. I've done very boring jobs, like cleaning bedrooms with room attendants, and I've done physically hard work in the kitchens. I didn't like the lower-level jobs, but I could see the point of knowing how to do them. I rotated through departments for six months, but it wasn't all routine. When the training manager thought that I had a grasp of the basics, I shadowed the heads of departments and saw what their responsibilities were. I gradually learned how to manage staff and saw how decisions were made.

After six months, I had a review with the hotel manager and the company's training manager. They concluded that I was ready for the next step, and I have now moved to a larger hotel in a different part of the country to work as a trainee assistant manager. Naturally, I have no living expenses so I can manage nicely. All through my training period I have to keep a training log. It records my training needs, how I am meeting them, my progress, comments from different section heads on my work, and some projects that I have had to complete. In this new job I am going to train to NVQ level 3, with help from the company's training officer who will visit me regularly and go through my training log with me.'

Jake

Retail management trainee with a national group

'I didn't consider the higher education option for very long after seeing what happened to my brother. He deliberately chose to do a degree that he thought would get him a good job – business studies – and worked really hard. He had to take out the full student loan every year *and* work every Friday night and all day Saturday in term time, just to keep his head above water and avoid having to borrow any more money. He hasn't been able to find a decent job. He's earning about £11,000 in an office job with the Civil Service, and still has his student loan to worry about. He's back at home with my parents and doesn't know when he'll be able to afford to move out.

I knew that I wanted to become a manager of some kind, and as soon as possible, so I asked my careers adviser for addresses of companies. It turned out that none of our big local ones ever took trainees, but she did mention retailing. I've always been interested in fashion, so when she mentioned this large group that includes most household names I was really interested. I applied and was successful.

I'm on what's known as a fast-track management training programme, and if I do OK I should be given my own small store at the end of 12 months. All my training is run by the company. I have a folder that lists all the things I should be learning in the branch (such as selling and staff recruitment) and I tick them and get my manager to sign them off as I become competent. I also have to spend four placements in other stores within the group, working as a deputy manager. I get good external training too. I go on short courses with other trainees who started at the same time as I did. We have studied buying and merchandising, and have done skills courses in leadership and management techniques.

I hope to be an area manager in five years – not paying off debts like my brother.'

Evening classes

Many people at work obtain professional qualifications for their job through attending evening classes, usually at a local further education college. Rachael, below, describes her experience of this.

Rachael

Legal executive

Rachael was named National Legal Executive of the Year 2005, by the Birmingham Law Society. Yet when she was doing her A level course in business studies and English literature, she had no idea that the career existed – let alone what it involved.

She knew that she wanted to earn and learn at the same time and considered both law and accountancy, knowing that both these professions offered part-time routes to qualification.

'I eventually decided on law, and applied for a job as a legal secretary at the firm where I still work. I knew that I would have to start at the bottom, and explained at the interview that although I could type and was ready to do routine work to begin with, I was ambitious and wanted to progress. The partner who was conducting the interview told me that the firm was very keen on developing its staff and would support me through the training and exams of the Institute of Legal Executives (ILEX). I didn't like to admit that I didn't know what ILEX was, so I went away and read about it.

I started as a legal secretary in the Claimant Personal Injury Department and began the college course after a few months. It was tough! I had to attend college one evening a week after a full day's work and do a lot of studying as well. It was recommended that students did the equivalent of one hour's study every day. I was very firm about this at first and kept myself to a strict timetable – but it doesn't work like that. There are other things to do and social life to think about! So I ended up doing the same amount of work, but using some time at weekends.

Meanwhile, at work, I was being given some files (cases) to handle. I was working by now in the Uninsured Losses Department and was given responsibility for handling clients' claims. My work was always checked by someone senior at first and signed off by them. Soon I was managing 50 files, and then I moved to working on personal injury claims. There I became a junior fee earner (the solicitors' term for staff who generate fee income as opposed to working in a support role) – and after a while I became the highest fee earner in the firm. I was very proud at this point, because I was bringing in more income than all of the solicitors and partners!

I continued to attend college and work for the exams, while at work I was given a bit more responsibility every six months or so. I never felt overwhelmed by this because it all followed naturally, building on what I could do and on what I was learning at college. I am now a fully qualified Fellow of the Institute of Legal Executives. I could, if I wished, begin to train as a solicitor, but I don't think that I shall do so. I have a very interesting job as a senior manager, and being a solicitor would not would not make any difference to my salary. I now oversee the supervision and operation of three teams, manage 18 fee earners, 15 support staff and a department that handles in excess of 5000 personal injury cases and has an annual turnover of £5 million. Changes to regulations in the legal profession mean that ILEX Fellows may be allowed to become partners in solicitors' firms, and with my firm's support I hope to be one of the first to achieve this.'

Part-time degree route

As previously mentioned, starting work at 18 does not necessarily mean you'll not progress onto higher education! You may have already read on page 42 about Michelle, whose training as an Advanced Apprentice has led her to starting a part-time engineering degree course, sponsored by her employer. Below we have an account of Tom, who is taking a part-time degree while working, as part of his company's training programme.

Tom

Trainee design coordinator with a major construction company

Tom is following his company's non-graduate management training scheme, which he started after completing an Advanced GNVQ (equivalent to a double-award A level) in construction and the built environment.

On starting work, Tom followed the company's induction training programme. This included finding out about the company and its facilities, communication processes, policies, procedures and conditions of employment. It also covered health and safety, job roles etc. The training also included various other introductory-level courses e.g. in health and safety, first aid, IT and team building.

Tom is training to be a design coordinator. His work involves going on site, talking to consultants, reviewing drawings in the office (e.g. to solve problems with designs) and attending meetings. He works four days a week and goes to university one day a week. The company's training scheme involves going on secondments to various internal departments. This has given Tom an awareness of the workings of the company, an understanding of careers within the industry, an appreciation of how his own role influences and impacts on others and a wider understanding of his own job.

In addition, Tom has attended some CITB trade awareness courses. This has helped him understand who does what on site, so that as a manager, he doesn't expect craftspeople to do unreasonable tasks.

At university, Tom is taking a BSc degree in construction management. This is through day-release over five years. He realises that he could have gone to university full-time, but his older sister had found the cost of full-time university study a strain. He felt that getting a job with training and going to university part-time would be better for him – he now gets a good salary, a company car and the added bonus that his company pays his university fees! Even more importantly, Tom is finding that his university course is giving him an insight into the industry and he is able to see the theory from his course put into practice at work.

Tom finds that it's good fun to be a student for one day a week – he gets to wear what he wants and enjoys the relaxed atmosphere. However, he says that studying by day-release can be tough – you work for four full days, have one day at university and then have to spend time studying at home. You have to be very determined to get your work out in the evenings because an assignment has to be in.

Performance permitting, at the end of the training scheme, Tom will be promoted to assistant design coordinator. He will finish his degree and complete his dissertation and then start an in-house management development scheme. By the time Tom completes his initial training, he will be well qualified and should have a good position within the industry.

Graduate Apprenticeships and Higher Apprenticeships

You might, just might, find that an employer offers to place you on a **Graduate Apprenticeship** (GA) programme.

These were developed under an initiative announced in 1998 by the Department for Education and Skills (DfES), and were intended to enhance the employment skills of new graduates. They combined existing higher education qualifications with work-based learning and NVQs. There was a pilot phase of GAs and subsequently, for a while, the scheme was widened. However, funding arrangements for the scheme altered, and funding became harder to obtain. A review in 2004 found that, without additional funding, it seems the remaining GA schemes might not be able to continue in the long term. So, *if* an employer were to mention GA programmes to you – you now know what they are!

The Sector Skills Councils (the bodies that now have responsibility for addressing the skills and learning needs of their sector of industry) are currently deciding whether they might offer **Higher Apprenticeships**. These have already been mentioned on page 36. Up and running, so far, are the ones in computing and IT under the auspices of e-skills UK, the Sector Skills Council for IT.

This is what e-skills UK says about the IT programmes.

'Higher Apprenticeships aim to provide a work-based degree route, which builds on the Apprenticeship by maximising HE recognition of the complex practical learning in the workplace at NVQ level 3, including the underpinning knowledge of the technical certificate and the personal and business awareness skills developed in the workplace for the Apprenticeship.

The new programme aims to establish joint delivery and assessment planning, where appropriate, between the Apprenticeship provider and the Higher Education Institution so that in existing HE and Apprenticeship courses, joint structures for assignments for academic credit and demonstrations of workplace competence could allow an IT apprentice realistically during the Apprenticeship to consider dual registration as apprentice and additionally as IT degree student.'

The Sector Skills Council for Science, Engineering and Manufacturing Technologies (SEMTA) is seriously considering introducing Higher Apprenticeships, and is asking employers whether they would like to see them introduced and, if so, what they would like to include in the content. The Higher Education Funding Council for England says that a number of other Sector Skills Councils have shown interest in Higher Apprenticeships.

You can obtain a list of the different Sector Skills Councils and their websites at www.ssda.org.uk – and check with the ones that cover the jobs that might interest you whether Apprenticeships are likely to be introduced. Alternatively, you could ask your Connexions personal adviser/careers adviser.

Finding out where the jobs are

You really need to start looking as early as the end of the autumn term of your final year. There are lots of sources and it pays to use as many as possible. Try:

- your careers adviser/Connexions personal adviser

- careers teacher

- school or college notice board (some employers send job advertisements in)

- advertisements in local newspapers

- sending speculative letters – i.e. writing to companies to ask whether they expect to have any vacancies in the job area that you want to enter (don't send too many of these – you could strike lucky, but equally you could become disheartened)

- the internet – this now carries a lot of jobs and careers sites – some of them are of limited use to school and college leavers and contain jobs for people with experience (try fish4jobs.co.uk)

- anyone you know who is already at work in the area that interests you and could tip you off about any jobs that are likely to come up (vacancies are often advertised first internally on staff notice boards).

And Apprenticeships

There are a number of ways to find out which Apprenticeships are on offer.

Your most likely source is a Connexions or careers service. If you have trouble finding your nearest office, your careers or guidance teacher at your school or college should be able to put you in touch.

You can call the national Apprenticeships helpline on 08000 150 600 (029 2090 6801 in Wales; 0845 8502 502 in Scotland; 0800 100 900 in Northern Ireland) and ask for more details about the areas of work you are interested in. It's a freephone number, so the call won't cost you anything. You'll then be sent some information. Within a few weeks, a local adviser will be in touch to set up meetings with learning providers near you. These learning providers have contacts with local employers who may have suitable vacancies.

You can apply for an Apprenticeship by going direct to employers who are offering Apprenticeships. They'll usually send you information about the training. Some larger employers have information about Apprenticeships on their websites.

You can check out local job listings, newspapers or listen to local radio stations.

Local recruitment agencies may also be able to help.

Life at work

It might be a bit scary at first. Everyone else seems to know exactly what they are doing. They all seem so mature. But you'll soon be OK.

They were all new once. The important thing is never be afraid to ask for help. It's far better to ask someone to explain something than to hope that you know what you are doing and make mistakes. In a large organisation you might start on the same day as other trainees and spend a day or more on an induction programme run by the human resources department. Induction usually covers an introduction to the company and what it does, presentations on their work from managers of different departments, information on courses and qualifications from a training officer, a talk on health and safety from a safety officer and details of your hours of work, lunch arrangements, what to do if you are ill and so on. It's a lot to take in. You might be given a folder with all the information in it. If not, once again, never be afraid to ask someone what you need to know. An induction programme in a large company might also include a tour of the building.

In a smaller organisation, you might be assigned to one person whose job it is to look after you and make sure that you know your way around and what is expected of you.

In both cases, someone will be put in charge of looking after your training and showing you the job.

If you join a big company you will probably be very lucky, because there is likely to be a social club which puts on lots of different activities from sports to pub nights, quizzes, theatre trips and even weekends away. You will find it an invaluable way to meet people – particularly those of your own age who work in other departments.

Problems?

You will be starting at the bottom and must remember not to be too impatient if you think you are being given all the boring jobs to do. You might have to put up with a bit of good natured teasing to begin with as well! It's not uncommon to send the new boy or girl off on a silly errand (which they may or may not spot) for instance.

Hopefully, you'll have an exciting and interesting experience – but if things don't quite work out what can you do? First – be patient and wait a while. Then sit down and make a list of points that you need to sort out – like training courses that are not happening, difficulties with a supervisor – whatever it is that is worrying you. Most people settle down OK, but remember you do not have to put up with anything like bullying. It can be difficult to report what is wrong, but you will need to muster up your courage to approach someone. It could be a friendly colleague to start with. Then you could go to your supervisor, line manager or to someone in the human resources department. You don't have to do this on your own. Talk it over at home, with friends – and if you would like to talk things over with a completely unbiased person go back to your Connexions or careers adviser. Things should be sorted out – but if not, you will have to look for another job. Once again – most people do not have problems.

Rights and responsibilities

Rights

Your contract

When you start work you have a *contractual agreement* with your employer. This should be given to you in writing soon after you start the job, but even if you don't have a written contract as long as you are paid for the work you do you still have this contractual agreement.

A contract contains the rights and obligations between yourself and your employer. If your employer breaches these, workers may be entitled to compensation. For instance, an employer should not change the hours of work against the terms of the contract without getting employees' consent. Employees, of course, are required to work the hours they are paid for and must not keep turning up late or leaving early. A contract will contain much more than this and will go into a lot of detail about pay, sick pay, holidays, rights to time off in certain circumstances etc. You will need to read it carefully – and to keep your copy somewhere safe.

Health and safety

Your health and safety at work is the responsibility of both you and your employer.

Holidays

Employees, including Apprentices are entitled to at least 20 days' paid holiday a year – but this can include the eight bank holidays. (This entitlement will be written into your contract.)

Minimum wage entitlement

You should receive a minimum amount of money per hour that you work, depending on your age. This is set by the Government and is known as the *minimum wage*. At present the rate for workers aged 18-21 is £4.25, with a proposed increase to £4.45 in October 2006. The hourly rate for workers aged 22 is £5.05, with a proposed increase to £5.35 in October 2006. The minimum wage entitlement does not apply though if you are doing an Apprenticeship. (But most employers pay apprentices at least the minimum wage.)

Sick pay

If you have to take more than four days off, you may be entitled to sick pay. The Government sets a minimum amount of sick pay you should receive, which is known as *statutory sick pay*. Some employers are more generous and pay over this minimum amount. Check this. It should be explained in your contract – together with information on what you do if you are sick (such as who to inform at your place of work).

Unfair dismissal

In order to make a claim for unfair dismissal, you have to have been in that job for at least one year. If an employment tribunal finds that you have been unfairly dismissed, you may be entitled to compensation.

The law

There are several laws to protect you. *The Employment Rights Act* covers your contract of employment, period of notice required on either side, right to join a union, unfair dismissal and redundancy pay.

The Health and Safety at Work Act requires employers to create a safe working environment. They have to ensure, for example, that office workers are provided with good light, suitable chairs and no-glare computer screens. In factories and laboratories, machinery must be guarded and dangerous substances stored properly. Construction workers must be provided with hard hats, safety boots, scaffolding and so on. Someone should be trained in first aid, and large organisations have occupational health centres staffed by doctors and specialist nurses who know all about occupational injuries and how to deal with accidents at work.

There are also laws to protect you against *discrimination* on the grounds of *disability*, *gender* or *race* – not as yet on age, sexual orientation or religion – although some legislation in these areas is being considered.

Responsibilities

These are not all one-sided. You will have obligations to your employer too. You must for instance:

- attend college regularly if you are enrolled on a course as part of your training

- complete any assignments that are required as part of your training

- let your manager or supervisor know if you are ill and unable to work

- take good care of any equipment that you use

- work the hours that are specified in your contract of employment (no turning up late without a good reason or sneaking off five minutes early every day).

Money

You will, rightly, get a thrill when you receive your first salary cheque or pay packet. You will probably also get a nasty shock when you see how much money has already disappeared from your total salary or wages!

You may be paid in cash in a wages envelope that shows the gross amount of your pay and the deductions that have been taken from it. Or your employer may pay your salary directly into your bank account, and at the end of each month you will receive a salary notification slip showing how much has been paid in for you – and again what deductions have been made. (So you might need to open a bank account.)

What are deductions? The two main ones are income tax and National Insurance contributions. There might also be deductions for contributions you choose to make to a pension fund if your employer offers one. (If you start work after leaving higher education you may find that deductions for repayment of tuition fees and a student loan have also been made, since the Government makes employers responsible for collecting these from you on their behalf.)

What is the difference between a salary and wages? Salaries are paid monthly, and wages weekly.

What you are left with is yours – but you will have expenses. You will need to budget for:

- fares to and from work
- lunches
- clothes – for work and social life
- rent, food and utility bills – unless you are living at home, in which case you might still be expected to pay for some of the cost.

Problems? Difficulties? Who can help?

If you have any problems at all with any aspect of work, you can seek help from the Connexions/careers services or from the Citizens Advice Bureau whose advisers are there to help anybody who has a problem relating to employment and much more (for example, consumer rights, housing or money problems).

Working for yourself

You might like the idea of being your own boss. It isn't easy to start out on your own – although some people do. (Most work for somebody else first, and make their mistakes at someone else's expense!)

If you think that you have a good business idea and the skills to run it, you can get further advice – and this includes the all-important advice on where to obtain finance – from some specialist organisations that help young people to set up on their own. Two relevant organisations are the Prince's Trust and Shell LiveWIRE.

The Prince's Trust

A charity that awards grants and low interest loans to people between the ages of 18-30 who can produce a realistic business plan and convince trust officials that they are committed and enthusiastic. In order to be eligible for assistance from the trust you would have to prove that you had tried all other possible sources of loans (for example, banks and your own family). The Prince's Trust is run through a network of local offices. You should be able to find the nearest one listed on the website, www.princes-trust.org or in the telephone directory. You can also find introductory information on how the trust works on the website.

Shell LiveWIRE

A national scheme, which encourages people aged 16-30 to become entrepreneurs. It was begun by Shell UK Limited in 1982, and since then has assisted over 180,000 young people with free local advice, information and business support for their ideas. You can find out all about it at www.shell-livewire.org or by phoning Shell LiveWIRE, 08457 573 252 (local call rate) and asking for an information pack.

You can find more information on both organisations, and case studies of some people who have successfully started their own businesses, in *Jobs and Careers after A Levels and equivalent advanced qualifications*, published by Lifetime Careers Publishing.

Busting the jargon

Block release

This means being sent by an employer for periods of several days, or even weeks, to attend job-related courses.

Day release

Spending one day each week at a college on a job-related course.

Distance learning

Studying at home in your own time, using study materials that are sent to you – or increasingly, are on the internet.

FE College

College of Further Education – which people may attend to obtain qualifications – through day-release, block-release or evening classes.

LSC

Learning and Skills Council. The organisation that funds work-related learning. It has regional offices.

MA

Modern Apprenticeship (Wales).

NVQ

National Vocational Qualification.

On-the-job training

Being taught how to do a job in the workplace by a senior colleague or manager.

Off-the-job training

Gaining skills and knowledge relevant to the job at a college of further education, or at an employer's or training organisation's premises.

SVQ

Scottish Vocational Qualification.

Chapter four
What is higher education?

Higher education (or HE) is the title given to courses that start at level 4. In other words, they are advanced courses which require level 3 qualifications (or other acceptable qualifications such as Access) for entry. The most usual ones are:

- A levels and AS levels

- Scottish Highers/Advanced Highers

- National Diplomas or Certificates

- Advanced GNVQ/GSVQ level 111 (both now replaced by newer qualifications, but still valid)

- NVQ or SVQ level 3.

Access courses are normally followed by people who have been out of education for some time and who need an alternative route to the other entry qualifications listed.

There are several different ways of obtaining a higher education qualification. The most popular is still the full-time option, but the number of part-time students is increasing rapidly – especially since the introduction of foundation degrees. (These will be explained later in this chapter.) According to the Department for Education and Skills, 43% of the 18- to 19-year-old age group now choose the full-time higher education route. The Government's aim is that by the year 2010, 50% of young people aged 18-30 should experience higher education – but no particular route for this is specified. If you add in the numbers of part-time students, it is possible that this target will be met.

Qualifications

What does HE offer?

One of the most common qualifications is the first degree. This is also known as a Bachelor's degree – and the title of it will vary according to the subject you do. The most common are BA (arts and humanities) and BSc (science) but there are also BEng (engineering) LLB (law) and MB or BMed (medicine) among others. Students may follow a first degree with a postgraduate diploma, a Master's degree or a Doctorate.

Honours degrees

In England, Northern Ireland and Wales most BA and BSc courses take three years of full-time study. In Scotland, they take a year longer because they include a more general first year. Courses that include professional training – such as architecture and medicine are always longer. *Sandwich* degree courses include periods of industrial training and experience and add at least a year to the course.

Honours degrees can be general (sometimes referred to as gateway courses – because they do not train you for a particular job but keep lots of options open for you). They can be strictly vocational – in other words they train you for a specific career at the end of the course, like radiography, medicine or social work. They can be in a job-related area – but not commit you to a specific career – for example, business studies.

You will have the choice of studying just one subject – single honours, a joint or combined programme, or a course that covers an area – like business studies or media studies, but which contains several different subjects within it. So you might do a single subject like geography, or take a course in an area like business studies, which includes different topics like accounting, human resources, marketing, business law, company finance and business information technology. Media studies could include radio, film, television, computing and the printed media, newspapers, journals and magazines.

You might choose for instance:

- BA business studies

- BA English literature

- BA French and Russian

- BA history with politics

- BSc physics

- BSc combined science

- BSc environmental science

- BSc geography with geology.

In most cases you'll be allowed to design the course to fit your own interests by choosing a number of modules each year. The first year often follows a set pattern, with mainly core or compulsory subjects plus a limited choice of options. Then as your interests develop in the next two years you get a bigger choice of options.

N.B. You may come across degree courses that offer a foundation year or year 0. These are generally in degrees in scientific subjects, and the foundation year is aimed at those who have not studied the right subjects at A level. Such courses should not be confused with foundation degrees (see below).

Foundation degrees

These have been around for about four years now and are becoming well known. They are, in any case, designed in consultation with employers. They are courses that train people in specialist skills for careers in areas like business, engineering, law – but there are over 100 different courses. In addition, all foundation degree programmes develop:

- work skills, relevant to a particular careers area

- key skills, for example communication and problem solving

- general skills such as reasoning and professionalism.

Students doing foundation degrees could have A2 and AS levels, GNVQs or NVQ level 3, and be students or Advanced or Modern Apprentices. You can study for a foundation degree full time, or through part-time or distance learning if you are in a job.

Foundation degrees are a qualification in their own right, and people with foundation degrees can use the letters 'FdA' (for arts-based subjects) or 'FdSc' (for science-based subjects) after their names. When you have gained a foundation degree, you'll be able to choose between working for professional qualifications in a job, or converting it into an honours degree through further study, usually by transfer into the second or third year of a degree course in a related subject area.

The length of foundation degree programmes varies – but a normal pattern is to take two years on a full-time basis; longer if part time.

BTEC Higher National qualifications

These have been around for a long time. The idea was that when foundation degrees were introduced that they would replace BTEC Highers. The Department for Education and Skills says that most

HNDs will be modified as necessary and converted into foundation degrees. This hasn't happened yet, although many institutions are now revising their course content and making the switch. In others, the two qualifications exist side by side.

BTEC is the Business and Technology Education Council – which joined the University of London Examinations Council to form Edexcel. BTEC offers Edexcel's job-related qualifications – in a wide range of areas. As with foundation degrees, you can do BTEC qualifications by studying full time or part time.

The programmes of study are roughly equivalent to the first two years of a Bachelor's degree programme. You can complete a diploma in a year less than it takes to do a degree. This means taking two years to do one on a full-time basis, and three years for a sandwich course.

Like foundation degrees, HNDs are always in vocational or job-related subjects. You won't find them in subjects like politics or English. There are currently over 80 BTEC HNDs, across 22 work-related sectors. Business, engineering, computing and IT are the currently most popular subjects.

When you finish an HND you can usually choose between getting a job and getting more training/qualifications while working, or doing a one year 'top-up' course if you decide you want to convert it to a degree. This doesn't apply just to universities in the UK. Edexcel says that the HND qualification can also be used to enter the third year of four-year Bachelor's degree at 29 universities in the USA and Australia.

Higher National Certificate (HNC) programmes are at the same standard as HNDs, but cover less ground since they contain fewer modules. For this reason, they are often taken part time by people already at work who choose the modules that are appropriate to their job. *But* full-time programmes are available.

For more information on HND and HNC programmes visit the Edexcel website, www.edexcel.org.uk

Diploma of Higher Education (Dip HE) programmes

A Dip HE is equivalent to the first two years of a degree. It can be a qualification in its own right, or can be used to give entry to the third year of a degree course. It is sometimes combined with professional qualifications. Nursing diploma courses, for example, normally lead to a Dip HE.

The Open University

If you're over 18 and you want to do a degree, but without becoming a full-time student, there is one more option to look into. The Open University (OU) is based in Milton Keynes in Buckinghamshire, but not many students ever go there. They study at home through distance learning, using course materials prepared by OU staff, and, if they can, they meet other OU students in study groups. You can choose from about 200 distance-learning degree courses, and if you have a level 3 qualification you will be able to skip the introductory course and enrol on the programme of your choice.

OU students study at their own pace. All courses are modular, so you can do one module at a time and build up your degree over the period of time that suits you. You will receive support from a tutor – in small, local study groups if you can get to one; by phone and e-mail if not. You will also be able to attend residential summer schools.

The OU offers 34 BA or BSc degrees, five foundation degrees and 35 diplomas.

An enormous range

As you have seen you can study a single subject, or more than one on a combined or joint programme. You can study something you have done at A level or at National Diploma level. You can also study something completely new. Architecture and veterinary science are obvious examples, as are all the subjects related to medicine – physiotherapy, dietetics, speech therapy, and so on. But have you any idea of just how many topics there are that you can start from scratch in HE? Here are just some of them. You can find more in the UCAS Directory or at the UCAS website:

acoustics	adventure	animal care and welfare
animation	anthropology	aromatherapy
astronomy	auctioneering/valuation	biodiversity
blacksmithing	book binding	calligraphy
Chinese	chiropratic	choreography
conflict studies	consumer science	commercial music
corporate communication	cosmetic science	cricket
globalisation	golf	rugby or tennis studies
criminology	deaf studies	digital arts/technology
disaster studies	e-business	engineering (including chemical, civil, electrical, electronic & mechanical)
entertainment	entomology	entrepreneurship
ergonomics	event management	evolution
feminist studies	fire safety	fishery science
fitness science	forensic science	genetics
gambling studies	gender studies	greenkeeping
herbal medicine	heredity	Hispanic studies
holistic therapy	internet studies	jazz
knowledge based systems	leadership studies	leather studies
logistics	meteorology	midwifery
motorsports	museum studies	neuroscience
Occitan	outdoor studies	paper science
perfumery	playwork	puppetry
quantum science	risk management	robotics
saddlery	screenwriting	scriptwriting
sound recording	space science	stage management
sustainable development	Third World studies	toxicology
travel	tunnelling	Ukranian
uniformed services	Victorian studies	virtual reality
war studies	waste management	watersport management
wine studies	yacht design	yarn technology
zoology		

Where can you study?

Higher education institutions fall into the following groups:

- *Universities* – these vary in size, from those with fewer than 4000 students to those with over 10,000. The largest run a wide range of courses. The smaller ones may have fewer subjects on offer – for example little or no science at some; no engineering at another. All universities offer honours degree programmes. Not all of them offer Diploma courses or foundation degrees. The universities that began life as polytechnics served the needs of local employers and designed courses relevant to particular industries. Today they run a wider range of programmes, including honours degrees, HNDs and foundation degrees.

- *Higher education colleges and institutes* – are smaller than the universities. Some run similar programmes to those in the universities – and most of them are applying or have applied to become universities. Others specialise in just a few subjects.

- *Specialist colleges* – there are a number of these, offering courses in just one area, for example, art, music, drama, agriculture.

You can apply to study at any university or college in the UK, no matter where you live.

Learning

There are several different methods used in higher education – some of which are used more in some subjects than in others. Depending on your subject of study you will find some combination of the following methods.

Lectures which are given to large groups of students – sometimes as many as 200 in a large lecture theatre. A member of staff gives a presentation (talk plus visual aids like overhead projector or PowerPoint) and students make notes. The setting is formal and there is usually no interaction between lecturer and students, although there may be an opportunity to ask questions at the end. Often, the lecturer hands out a summary of the lecture and a reading list.

Seminars are held for smaller groups – perhaps up to 16 students, and are more like classes in a school or further education/sixth form college, with a lot of student participation. Often they are based on a previous lecture and are an opportunity for all the students to make sure that they understand the topic. Sometimes they cover points raised in the lecture or on the students' reading list. Other types of seminar are led by students who make a short presentation on a topic they have been allocated. This is then discussed by the whole group with some input from a lecturer.

Practicals (science courses) – these consist of laboratory work, exercises done on computer, and individual and group projects – again often based on a previous lecture. You might do some practicals on your own, or often with two or three other students.

Practicals (art and design, performing arts and media courses) – these could consist of anything from working up a brief for a fashion design, to holding group rehearsals for a play, to carrying out projects in recording and film studios. Again, you would do some of them in a small group or team and might also have some individual projects to do.

Presentations – it is very common, particularly on vocational courses like business studies, but also on academic ones like geography or environmental studies, for a small group of students to be given an assignment to do. They decide between themselves how to divide up parts of the work, research their own part, then produce a joint report which they present (usually taking a topic each) to a larger group of students – and one or more members of staff.

Problem classes – these are rather like tutorials and are held mainly in science and technological subjects. Students will previously have been given a worksheet and now meet to discuss their answers.

Supervisions or tutorials – these are discussion based and are rather like seminars, although more used on science courses. A group of students meet regularly with a member of staff and work together. The topic might be based on a lecture or on a practical. Group numbers vary at different institutions. They could consist of 6-15 students.

Tutorials (another meaning) – traditionally a tutorial was a one-to-one meeting between a student and a tutor, in which the student would read out a prepared essay. The tutor would then comment and criticise, and both would discuss. This method is still used in Oxbridge colleges. At other places a tutorial can mean a smaller group than a seminar – perhaps up to 12. The structure is similar – discussion based and often led by a student. The definitions of seminar and tutorial vary from institution to institution, and sometimes even within departments at the same one.

Assessment

There are various assessment methods, and many institutions use a combination. Very few places now rely on final exams alone. Many hold yearly exams and/or tests at the end of each module. The marks for these are added to marks from any forms of continuous assessment that may be used, and all of them put together determine the grade of your final qualification. Continuous assessment may include:

- essays

- laboratory reports

- practical work (for example art and design projects, or performances for creative arts students)

- fieldwork reports

- worked projects

- assignments

- a dissertation – a long essay which contains original research, often done in the final year (at some places it is called a *project* or *thesis* – although the term thesis is more usually applied to a postgraduate research project).

Study routes

Full time

Studying 'full time' does not mean that you would sit in classes from 9am to 5pm every day, or even that you would have the same number of hours of formal teaching or class contact time as you do at school or college. The number of hours of timetabled work that you have on a full-time programme will depend on your degree subject. Some subjects, like engineering, have as many as 20 hours; some humanities subjects as few as five hours! However, you will be expected to put in a lot of hours of work on your own on courses that do not include much teaching time. You will be expected to spend time reading around lecture topics, and in research and reading in order to write essays (which may then form the basis of a seminar group discussion).

Humanities and social science students tend to have the lowest number of lectures, but are expected to spend a lot of hours in the rest of the week in private study. They have essays, assignments and presentations to prepare, and may choose to work at home or in the university or college library. Science and engineering students have more hours on their timetable because they have to attend laboratory and practical classes. They too will have some work to do in their 'free' time, however. Students on some other courses will also have to put in additional hours – language students in language laboratories and conversation classes, and geography students on residential field trips, for example.

The academic year usually lasts for 30-32 weeks, and is either broken into three terms or two semesters. Oxford and Cambridge are the exceptions, having three very short terms of eight weeks. You can expect breaks, known as vacations, at Christmas and Easter, but not normally half-term holidays. If you choose a course which has end-of-term examinations, these will usually take place at the end of May and the beginning of June. You then have a long summer in which to work (most students have to do this to help with their budgets) and possibly do some travelling.

Part time

There are many variations on part-time courses. Some institutions run part-time evening courses. Others use a day, or the equivalent of one whole day, a week. Arrangements are often made locally by individual subject departments, which work with local employers and bear their needs in mind. In other words, if the town's largest employer gives its employees day release to attend classes then these will probably be organised over one long session – a day stretching into the evening. Sometimes it is possible to start a course following one pattern and switch to another if circumstances change.

You can read the accounts of Tom, who is taking a degree course on a part-time basis while working, and Michelle, whose employer is about to sponsor her through a part-time degree, in Chapter three (pages 42 and 59).

Distance learning

This takes place whenever students find it convenient to study! Some prefer to set aside a certain number of weekday evenings, while others work better at weekends. If you choose the Open University, there would also be some short residential courses – normally summer schools.

Sandwich courses

Students often think 'I couldn't do a sandwich course. I am not going to do a science subject.' Sandwich courses, however, are not just for engineers and technologists. Language students often spend one academic year abroad; medical students and student teachers spend periods in clinical work or school placements. These placements, though, are a compulsory and necessary part of the course. Voluntary sandwich placements are available in most vocational courses including business studies, computing, food science, marketing, hotel management, finance, surveying – and even in some academic ones. Politics' students at some universities have the option to work for a British MP or US senator. Other placements can be with large companies like IBM – or with much smaller organisations.

Warning – some placements may be unpaid, and are strictly speaking work experience placements.

Students who are sponsored by industrial or business employers may find that they follow a *thick* sandwich programme, spending one whole year with their sponsoring organisations – often, but not always, the third year of the course – or a *thin* programme, which includes two or more periods of practical training of six to nine months each. Part of the summer vacation before or after the sandwich placement is usually included. This makes up the time spent with the employer to one full year or more.

What a sandwich course gives you is real, hands-on experience in a job to back up all the things that you are learning on your university or college course, and to counter some employers' argument that students graduate without any experience of working life. The experience should also help you to understand more clearly some of the topics that are taught on the course. When you qualify and are making job applications you will be so much more employable (not to mention mature) as a result of your work experience, and will be able to answer interview questions using examples from your placement.

These are the main advantages of doing a sandwich course but there are others. One very real one is that many students are offered employment by the firm where they did the placement.

There are some financial drawbacks to sandwich courses, though. You will need to balance these against the positive factors before you make your choice. First, you will be adding a year to your course. That's fine if you get a placement that pays enough to live on – but if you end up taking out more in a student loan to pay for the year it begins to look less attractive. Second, you will probably have to continue paying fees – at a lower rate – to your university or college during the placement.

Some students describe how their courses are structured

Jon

First-year student, foundation degree, electrical and electronic engineering (full-time)

'I did a two-year National Diploma in engineering at a college that has links with this one and several others. My main reason for choosing this particular one was that I liked the thought of small numbers of students. I have friends in big universities who are in lecture groups of 200 but I am in classes of 15.

On some days we are taught with part-time students who come in one day a week from local companies. On Mondays I am at college from 9.15am until 8pm – because these are the hours that the part-timers have to do on their college day. On Fridays we also work with part-time students, but for a slightly shorter day. On Thursday classes are from 9.15am until 5pm and are for practicals. I enjoy these. They take four hours (with a short break in the middle). I don't have any timetabled classes on Tuesday or Wednesdays, and I like having Tuesday completely free because I can choose to work at home or come into college. I often go in to use the library and all the other facilities, but on some days I stay at home. (I live with my parents.) Every Wednesday I work at the local leisure centre as a fitness instructor. They have been very good to me there. I started working as an unqualified assistant doing mainly physical work like setting up equipment and cleaning changing rooms, but the manager offered me the opportunity to work for some NVQs which I have done. I now work for the centre in the morning and evening, and in the afternoons I am allowed to use it for training sessions with my own clients. I have built up a list of people who want to work with a personal trainer. The income I earn each week helps out, because my parents cannot afford to give me any money – although, obviously, the free board and lodging is a big saving.'

Rob

First-year student, BA Hons English (full-time)

'My time is divided between four different courses – 'Explorations in literature', 'The short story', 'Literature 1895-1920' and 'Approaches to literature'. I have one lecture and one seminar every week. Seminars are discussion groups for eight or nine students. They always follow a lecture and are led by the person who gave it. We have had some really good ones. Two that stand out were on *King Lear*, which we had all done for A level and so there were lots of different views – and another on Thomas Hardy that linked *Jude the Obscure* with some of his poetry.

We are given essential reading before each lecture; also secondary reading. It would be impossible to read everything on that list so you have to decide what to choose.

When I first saw my timetable I couldn't believe it! Eight hours! Reality soon struck. I have to read for at least four hours each week to prepare for the lectures and seminars. I do a lot of this at night, because this is how I have always worked. Most of my time, however, goes on work for essays. I was given a list at the beginning of term, so I know when they are all due in. I have to spend whole days reading, and just before a deadline I spend several days putting all my notes together – then writing until the essay is done.

Having such a lot of 'free' time means that you have to learn to be self disciplined and to manage your own time. These are two of the skills that university teaches you. Sometimes I wonder where the week has gone. I have had to learn to fit in all my academic work, do my laundry – and shop and cook. (I am in a self-catering hall.) And I have an amazing social life. Everyone does.'

Amy

Second-year student, BA Hons French and Russian (full-time)

'In the first year, everyone does an introductory course in French culture and history. This makes a change from just focusing on the language, and also introduces you to the options you can choose throughout the course. These include linguistics, history, literature, cinema, art, politics and philosophy.

Seminars run alongside the lecture programmes, and last year we had 16 hours' timetabled lectures and seminars. Numbers for courses vary. The introductory French history course had over 100 students, my option modules around ten, language classes twelve, and oral classes four.

Obviously, we all take language modules covering written, oral and listening skills. These are largely taught by French nationals, and since they are young and in touch with today the lessons are interesting and up to date.

There are only 15 of us doing Russian. In the first year we had a very intensive language course with both written and oral classes. We also had an introductory course in history and literature. Options in Russian history and literature started this year.

A year abroad is compulsory after your second year. Since I started Russian from scratch, I'll probably be spending most of mine at a university in Moscow. Placements in France are usually working as an assistant in a school.'

Ian

Second-year student, BSc Hons physiotherapy (full-time)

'The first year was more lecture-based than I expected, but you need to know the underlying anatomy and physiology of structures before you investigate things more deeply and get hands-on experience in smaller seminar groups. We often have twenty hours a week of lectures and seminars, but they don't cover everything and a lot of the course involves directed study where you read and teach yourself. It's hard work and you must be self-motivated.

In my first year I had five weeks out on placement looking at how to communicate with patients, and how to manoeuvre them safely, for example, from beds to wheelchairs. My first placement was with children with learning disabilities; the second with elderly patients with strokes, or hip and knee replacements. Good communication skills are vital in our work.

The second year has been much more hands-on treatment and is more focused. I've just had practical and written exams and assessment, and now, for the next five weeks, I'm assessing and treating cardio-respiratory patients in a hospital ward. My supervisor is there to give advice and ask questions, but by the end of this placement it will just be me and my patients.'

Ruth

First-year student, foundation degree in criminology and criminal justice (full-time)

'We do a range of subjects including criminal justice, forensic psychology, principles of criminology, criminal law, victimology, mediation and new approaches to crime, plus research methods. I haven't studied them in much depth yet, but what I have done so far has been really interesting. Some of the module titles were new to me. 'Victimology' means looking at things from the victims' point of view.

There are 12 of us on the course and I see this as a real benefit. We can discuss things and ask questions if we don't understand. This is what I like. I would hate large lecture groups. I remember things much better if I have interacted with other people rather than simply made notes.

We have assignments for each module. One of the first, for the research module, involved conducting a survey and drawing up the conclusions. I chose to ask society's opinion of the nature/nurture debate with reference to criminals (in other words whether they are born with criminal tendencies or whether they acquire them as they are brought up). I have also done an assignment, which involved compiling a forensic profile of someone who had committed some unsolved rapes and murders, based on information we were given on the facts of the case as known.

We have some very interesting outside speakers! Some have come from the Police Force, the Youth Offending Team and Victim Support. One was an ex-convict who had spent more than 25 years in prison, he told us his views on the criminal justice system and described the changes he had seen in prisons during that time. He maintained, though, that he was innocent and should never have been there.

We are all required to gain some work experience. Some people already have relevant backgrounds, but I am one of the youngest on the course and so have had to find some. I decided to do voluntary work and now work in victim support. I spent four days on a training course, and now get about one referral a week. I have to do this work in the evenings or at weekends – to fit in with the client's hours.'

An international perspective

Many UK students now spend part of their higher education courses studying in another European country. They are not all modern languages students. So why do they do so?

■ Many employers now see the value of recruiting graduates with language skills.

■ Employment has become global. Companies have branches in many countries worldwide, and although English is an international language day-to-day business may be carried out in other languages.

■ Anyone resident in the European Union has the right to work in any other Member State. UK graduates are therefore competing for jobs with students from other countries – who often speak two or more languages well.

■ By spending part of their higher education courses in another country, British students can become fluent in other languages.

You could look for a summer vacation job in another EU country as you are entitled to do. You could even do your entire higher education course in another country (but there are likely to be both linguistic and financial difficulties in doing this – grants and loans are unlikely to be available). Alternatively, you could take part in the Erasmus programme – an option for full-time students.

The Erasmus programme

Erasmus (*'European Community Action Scheme for the Mobility of University Students'*) is a European Union programme set up to encourage students to study in another country, learn something about the culture, and improve their language skills.

You can spend from three to twelve months abroad studying almost any subject, and can include a work placement provided that you spend at least three months in academic study. The most popular subjects are business studies and engineering, but performing arts students, planners, historians and scientists can also take part. In fact, it is possible to arrange a placement in almost any subject. So, you could spend part of your maths course in Italy, your art course in Spain, your history course in France… etc. It is even possible to study in English by going to certain universities in Scandinavia or the Netherlands, but if you did that your progress in learning the language would be limited.

Places are available in all EU countries plus Bulgaria, Iceland, Lichtenstein, Norway, Romania and Turkey. (The EU countries are Austria, Belgium, Cyprus, Czech Republic, Denmark, Estonia, Finland, France, Germany, Greece, Hungary, Ireland, Italy, Latvia, Lithuania, Luxembourg, Malta, Poland, Portugal, Slovakia, Slovenia, Spain, Sweden, The Netherlands and The United Kingdom.)

Your own university or college would make the arrangements – and should also set up some language tuition for you before you went (especially if you were a beginner!). The host university would be responsible for arranging a programme of study for you, including lectures relevant to your study at home, plus language classes – and accommodation, although sometimes students do not know where they will be staying until after they arrive!

The period abroad counts for assessment towards your degree, and takes part during your normal degree course – i.e. with no additional time necessary.

If you receive financial support for a UK course you should be able to continue to have it paid while you are studying elsewhere if the study is part of your UK course. In addition, you would not have to pay tuition fees to your UK university or college while you were studying outside the UK, and might even be eligible for additional allowances to cover the extra expense you would incur.

If a university department has links with partner institutions in other countries it normally states this in the prospectus.

Student life

Being a student isn't all work. Far from it. You will be able to have a whale of a social life too – and it needn't cost the earth. Getting into clubs, eating and drinking in pubs and restaurants at reduced prices, all become possible when you are in possession of a student ID card. That's for activities outside the university or college. On campus you should be able to participate in a wide range of sports and fitness activities from team sports to using a gym – all at subsidised prices. But also, the cheaper forms of entertainment will be on campus where there will be gigs, discos, films, etc at reduced prices too. These will be organised by something that might play an important part in your life – the Students' Union. Unions are not just political organisations, although they do represent students and lobby for them in their own institutions and nationally. A union normally has a budget, which it can use to give grants to student clubs and societies.

Joining a society is a way of following up an interest and meeting new people, but it might surprise you to know that careers advisers and employers actively encourage students to join them. What you do in your leisure time can actually be useful? Yes. When you ultimately come to complete job application forms there will be spaces where you have to list your spare time activities – and more importantly, what you gained from them. So spare time activities can actually enhance your CV. This is not to say that anyone will be impressed by a list of memberships from the Jazz Club to the Tiddlywinks Society. (Yes, they do exist.) What you will be expected to do is give examples of the skills you have learned from being in these societies (for example working in teams, managing funds, organising your time to fit around the need for weekly rehearsals, etc). It would be better still if you could say that you had had a committee role or organised activities.

When you enrol at your HE institution you will be invited to something known as the Freshers' (that's you) Fair, or similar title. There you will find representatives from all the societies, dying to sign you up and relieve you of a membership subscription. *Don't* join too many. You'll blow your budget that way and, as societies are pretty intensive, you would soon find that you did not have time to make good use of them all.

What could you do? One university lists the following activities in its prospectus:

- African Caribbean Society
- Amnesty International
- Arab Society
- Archaeology Society
- Asian Society
- Astrosoc
- Ballroom and Latin American Dancing Society
- Band Society
- Big Band Society

- CAMRA
- Catholic Society
- Change Ringers
- Cheerleading Society
- Chess Society
- Chinese Society
- Choral Society
- Christian Union
- Circus Society
- Classical Music
- Conservative Future
- Cyprus Society
- Debating Society
- Duke of Edinburgh's Award
- Economics Society
- EMMAUS
- Engineering Society
- English Society
- Film Society
- Football Supporters Society
- Free Tibet Campaign
- Friends of Falungong
- Games Society
- Geography Society
- Geology Society

- Hindu Society
- History Society
- Ideological Society
- Investors
- Islamic Society
- Italian Society
- Japanese Animation Society
- Jedi Society
- Jewish Society
- Labour
- Law Society
- Liberal Democrats
- Malaysian Society
- Mass Communications Society
- Maths Society
- Modern Dance Society
- Modern Languages Society
- Museum Studies Society
- Navigators
- Orchestra
- People and Planet
- Personal Computing Society
- Photographic Society
- Poetry Society
- Politics Society

- Psychology Society
- Public Speakers' Society
- Rock Society
- Saudi Students Society
- Scandinavian Society
- Sci-Fi and Fantasy Society
- Sikh Society
- Singapore Society
- Small Black Flowers
- Socialist Students
- Sociology Society
- Street Jazz Society
- Student Action for Refugees
- Student Newspaper
- Symphonic Concert Band
- Taiwanese Society
- Travel Society
- Turkish Society
- Umoja Gospel Choir
- Vikings.

Plus – many different types of volunteer work in the local community and over 70 sports including:

- badminton
- dri ski
- fitness training

- golf

- riding

- rifle shooting

- sailing

- squash

- tennis

- windsurfing

- and all major team sports.

All of these activities will be open to full- and part-time students and those living at home.

Student support services

Also available to all students – but some likely to be of more interest to those who are living away from home – will be a range of student support services. You won't be left to sink or swim on your own, and if you do have any problems there will be people to help. Who are they?

Personal tutor

A member of teaching staff who looks after a number of students. He or she may be your first source of advice. If a problem is beyond their scope they know where to refer students. Some are better at dealing with academic work problems rather than personal or emotional ones. After all, they are not trained counsellors. Any student who feels uncomfortable discussing personal problems with someone who teaches them can go straight to the experts providing the services.

Welfare officer

Someone who can help with queries on housing, legal matters, discrimination, drugs, alcohol, etc. You could find that there are welfare staff employed by the university *and* by the Students' Union.

Study skills tutor

It might take you a little while to adjust to lots of free time, new teaching and learning methods – being responsible for your own time. If you need help in taking lecture notes, planning essays, or simply in time management, they are there to help. Some counsellors run group sessions. Others offer individual help.

Financial counsellors

Specialist advisers who can advise on budgeting and make sure that you know of all possible sources of extra help, like scholarships, hardship loans, grants to students in special need, and so on.

Personal counsellors

They can be consulted in confidence about *anything* – relationship problems, eating disorders, difficulties with the landlord, money worries, homesickness (yes – it happens!), depression and any other personal problems that might crop up.

Nightline

A listening service staffed all night, often by (trained) students. If you didn't need to use this service you might like to consider training for the work. Something else to put on your future job application forms!

Health and medical matters

If you are away from home you will probably be relieved if your university or college has a medical centre staffed by doctors and nurses. (Not all do.) If it has one, you will be invited to register there. Where there is no medical centre it is advisable to register with a local doctor. It would be difficult to arrange a home visit otherwise. (You can still consult your own doctor at home in the vacations.) If you are going to live at home you will probably wish to stay as a patient of your current doctor.

Chaplains

Most places have chaplains, of all denominations and faiths, who have chosen to work in higher education because they relate to the student age group.

Speakers representing all of these services will probably give short presentations about their roles during the 'Welcome' programme (sometimes known as Freshers' Week).

If you live in a hall of residence you may find that a number of senior students have been appointed 'sub-wardens'. They are volunteers who, usually in return for cheaper rent, have offered to act as student counsellors. They are specially trained and are there to help any students on an individual basis, also to represent the students and put their views to hall managers. (This is another CV enhancing role!)

Beating the jargon

As soon as you start to look on websites and read prospectuses, you will come across some terms that crop up time and time again. You might know some of them; others possibly not. Here are some definitions.

Academic year

Similar to the school year. In higher education it may start in either September or October. It normally finishes in late May or in June.

Bursary

A sum of money awarded to a student by a university or college. The word is often interchangeable with scholarship. There will be certain requirements or conditions attached. For instance, they might be given to new students with outstanding A level results, or for musical or sporting ability. Universities and colleges that charge more than £2700 per year tuition fees are also required by the Government to award bursaries of at least £300 per year to students who receive the full maintenance grant. Some bursaries are awarded by charities or professional bodies.

Catered hall

A hall of residence in which students have their own rooms (or sometimes share) and have some meals provided. Patterns vary, and could be breakfast and evening meal; breakfast, evening meal and weekend lunches; or all meals every day.

Combined studies

A course in more than one subject – often three. It may be possible to study as many as five – by taking different subjects in different years of the course.

CUKAS

Conservatoires UK Admissions Service. A special admissions system for places at certain music colleges, administered by UCAS.

Dissertation

An extended essay, or in-depth research project. It may replace one or more final examination papers and count for a significant % of marks. Some courses include a compulsory dissertation; others allow students to choose whether to do one.

ELB

Education and Library Board. In Northern Ireland, it has the same role regarding financial support for students as that of an English or Welsh LEA.

Fresher

A new student is known as a fresher at many places – usually for the first term. All sorts of activities are organised for new students at the beginning of the academic year, such as the 'Freshers' Fair', where student societies compete for new members and representatives of student services, like counsellors, chaplains, careers advisory services, welfare officers, etc, give presentations explaining what help they can offer if necessary.

Graduate

A student who has successfully completed a degree course and been awarded a degree is known as a graduate. He or she has graduated.

Joint degree

A degree in two subjects. They may (depending on the college or university) be of equal weight or studied in a major/minor combination.

LEA

Local Education Authority. Students in England and Wales apply to their own LEA in plenty of time (preferably in January of year 13) for financial assistance – i.e. help with payment of tuition fees and assessment of their entitlement to a student loan.

Lecturer

A member of academic staff in a higher education institution. The term does not mean that they do no other work than give lectures. They also conduct tutorials, seminars etc. In other words they are teachers. In addition to teaching undergraduate students they may also teach postgraduates and conduct research into their subject.

Maintenance grant

Students may apply for grants up to a maximum of £2700 per year. The grant is based on family income. The Government says that about half of all full-time students can expect to receive *some* grant. See Chapter seven for more details.

Module

A familiar term? A modular course is divided into separate areas of study. Students are assessed at the end of each one, and the marks are collected to form the final degree or Diploma grade. Most courses contain both compulsory and optional modules.

NMAS

The Nursing and Midwifery Admissions Service. Based in Cheltenham, this organisation handles applications to non-degree courses – i.e.

Diploma courses in both nursing and midwifery. (Degree course applications are made through UCAS.)

NUS

National Union of Students. This organisation negotiates nationally with Government on behalf of students and also provides a number of services to students. Nearly all Students' Unions are affiliated to it. With an NUS card you can get valuable discounts from shops, cinemas, clubs and travel operators.

Postgraduate

A student who has completed a degree and is now undertaking further study – on a Diploma course, or for a higher degree such as an MA, MSc or PhD.

Programme

Another word for a course – for example a programme of study, a degree programme.

SAAS

The Students' Awards Agency for Scotland. This organisation deals with financial support for Scottish students. There is more information in Chapter seven.

Sandwich course

A course that includes one year's planned work experience. It may consist of one placement or of two, each lasting six months and spent with different employers. Some sandwich placements are available overseas.

Scholarship

Some universities and colleges use this term to describe the same financial assistance as that given under a bursary. Usually however, scholarships are awarded for reasons other than a student's income. See chapter seven for more information.

Self catering accommodation

A hall of residence, or block of student flats, where students pay a lower rent than in a catered hall and cook for themselves.

SLC

The Student Loans Company. This organisation makes payments to students after their entitlement has been calculated by their LEAs. The SLC calculates loan repayments due when students have graduated and informs the Inland Revenue, which collects them.

Sponsorship

An arrangement under which an employer or other organisation pays a student a sum of money (sometimes known as a bursary) while they are at university. Some sponsors support students all the way through their courses. Many, though, prefer to take second- or final-year students. See Chapter seven for further information.

SU

The Students' Union – an organisation run by students for students. The SU receives some funding from the university or college, and makes more by charging students to attend events or use some of the facilities. The SU plays an important part in most students' lives. It funds many clubs and societies – from sports and social, to political and cultural. It often also arranges for students to do voluntary work in the local community. The SU also runs entertainments – gigs, discos, films, etc – at reasonable cost, provides student welfare services, and runs what is in effect a large business with bars, shops, coffee shops etc. It often employs full-time staff and offers part-time work to students. Student Union officers are elected by students.

Tutor

A member of teaching staff. At some places it can mean just that – a lecturer. But the word often describes a personal tutor – a lecturer who looks after a small number of students who may go to him/her with any kind of problem, academic or personal. Tutors know where to refer the student if the problem is outside their expertise.

UCAS

The Universities and Colleges Admissions Service. Based in Cheltenham, UCAS handles the administration connected with applying for higher education places. Students apply for places on a

UCAS form (online) which allows them up to six choices. UCAS also publishes a number of books in cooperation with different publishers and has its own website – which is a good place to start looking for any information connected with higher education.

Undergraduate

A student who has not yet graduated – i.e. a first-, second- or third-year (or a fourth-, fifth- or sixth-year on some courses – for example medicine).

Chapter five
Finding out

It obviously makes sense to find out as much as you can about the various options. How?

Careers, employment and training

You have probably had a work experience placement further back in your school career. Did it help? Maybe you enjoyed it; maybe you didn't. Whereas many students find the time spent in a workplace is valuable, some feel disappointed. If this happened to you, perhaps it was because you couldn't get your first choice of placement – in the job you really wanted to try out. (It can be very difficult for school staff to fit everyone in where they want to go if the whole year group goes out at the same time.) Never mind. Without realising it, you probably gained some insights into work in general that will be of help when you come to apply for a real job. You'll be able to refer to them on an application form, and talk about them at interview. These are things like observing how people worked together in teams or on projects, how different managers and supervisors treated people, and aspects of health and safety.

However, you might have the opportunity to have another try this year. If you are in year 12 or the first part of year 13, why not see what you can organise? If you do it on an individual basis, with or without help from school or college, you might be able to sort something for the Christmas or half-term holidays. There should be fewer people around looking for placements at these times. If the experience is good, you'll be confirmed in your choice of the type of job or Apprenticeship to apply for the end of year 13.

Work experience will be useful too, if you plan to apply for certain full-time courses in higher education. It's practically impossible, for instance, to get a place on a degree course in medicine and the caring professions (social work, teaching, medicine, dentistry or veterinary work) or those professions related to medicine (like physiotherapy and occupational therapy) unless you have worked with, and talked to, people in the profession and can talk about your experiences when you apply for the place. For entry to courses leading to other careers, like agriculture, surveying, law and town planning (to name but a few), you would be expected to have taken steps to find out what is involved in the career.

For many of these careers something called work shadowing is actually more appropriate than work experience. You, obviously, can't have a go at setting a broken limb, defending someone on a criminal charge, or auctioneering antiques. But you can spend time with the people who do the jobs and watch closely (with clients'/patients' permission where necessary). People who are being shadowed are usually very keen to explain what they are doing and allow you to ask questions – so it isn't a case of simply sitting there like a fly on the wall or feeling in the way.

Incidentally, if you decide that the full-time higher education option is for you, you may find that work experience is offered to you again. It will be almost certainly provided on courses that are career directed like journalism, environmental management and certain types of business course (such as human resources, accountancy or marketing). Since most foundation degrees are related to career areas, many of these include it too. Students on courses where work experience is not offered often arrange to spend part of the holidays shadowing or gaining work experience to help them when they eventually come to apply for a job – just as you might do now. In other courses, work experience is a compulsory part of the course. Students on courses related to medicine must do a set number of hours' clinical experience and student teachers must do teaching practice.

Gareth

Wants to work in the legal field

'I'm not sure whether I want to be a barrister or a solicitor yet. My careers teacher told me that I will be able to do a mini-pupillage in a barristers' chambers if I go to university, so suggested that I spent some time with a local firm of solicitors in year 12. She gave me some names and addresses, but I had to write and ask if they could help me. I spent a week there in the spring half term and had a really good time. I was allowed to sit in with one solicitor all day and see what kind of work he did on office days. There was quite a variety of clients – some wanting to draw up wills or powers of attorney for an elderly relative, one person who wanted to claim for unfair dismissal, and some who had problems with landlords or tenants. (That was interesting, seeing both sides.) One of the partners took me with her to the magistrates' court for a morning, where she was representing someone accused of a mugging, and I spent a whole day at the county court with another partner who was doing family work. In the office I met someone whose job I hadn't heard about – a legal executive. He was part-qualified and told me how he intended to work right up to becoming a solicitor. That sounded very interesting to me and I'm going to look into it further. I'm not 100% convinced that I want to go to uni full time and this could be an alternative way of training in law.'

Higher education

There are lots of ways of getting information on university and college courses – some more useful than others!

Most students start with the internet. Most universities and colleges have their own websites. These are fine if you already have some idea of where you might like to go, but what if you haven't? If you are still at the stage of choosing a course, a good place to begin is with the UCAS website, www.ucas.com It has a complete list of all the single subject and combined course that you can do within the UCAS system; links to university and college websites where you can check entrance requirements and then move on to look up details of their facilities; and a link through to a special site on foundation degrees. The UCAS site also has a lot of introductory information on student life and finance.

A point worth noting is that on individual websites you should find something called 'Entry profiles'. These are under individual courses, and describe the personal skills, qualities and experience you may need before starting the course, and how they will be developed during it. They are not available for all courses – but where they are they are very good, and can be a big help in your decision making.

Then there are prospectuses. You don't need dozens now that there are good websites – but it's useful to have some. You could read a uni website first and look at the details of the course, accommodation and other facilities – then request a selection of hard copy prospectuses from a shortlist of places that attract you most. Having hard copies is a good idea. You can make notes on them, and compare them with each other more easily than continually flicking between websites or printing off a forest of paper. Surveys show that students still regard these as one of the best information sources. They are especially good for information on the facilities the institution can offer – including accommodation – possibly a major factor in your choice. They also contain an outline of each course – although you will often find out more from specific course leaflets. Although your school or college will have reference copies it's better to get your own. Many schools have arrangement with an organisation that delivers bulk copies of prospectuses. All you have to do is get a form, put your name and address on it, and tick the ones you want. They should then come direct to your home address. Alternatively, you can order them online.

Warning – prospectuses are marketing tools and the sun is always shining in the photographs. (Colleges and universities want students don't they?)

If you can – perhaps on an organised visit with other students from your school or college – do go to a higher education convention. They are held at exhibition centres in major cities – and there should be one within travelling distance. If no visit is organised you can go alone or with friends or parents. You can meet representatives from different universities and colleges there and ask any questions you have. (Make a list first.) If the representatives can't answer some of the questions they usually take names and addresses and send the answer afterwards. It's a good idea to get a list of institutions that will have representatives attending beforehand. You could have a wasted journey if the ones on your list aren't going to be there. But you could still find the day useful, because there are usually some information sessions included. You should be able to attend talks given on topics like applications and student finance.

And as soon as you can – try to get to some university and college open days. There is no substitute for seeing a place for yourself. After all, you are planning to spend several years of your life there. At many open days there are now a number of separate tours and talks for students and parents. (Yes, it is quite OK to go with your parents! And they can provide transport too.) Higher education staff understand that parents have a lot of concerns – mainly about money, since they might be making a large contribution to your costs – and put on sessions at which they can answer questions. Meanwhile, you can be on a campus tour looking at the Students' Union building, sports facilities and halls of residence. Another word of warning. Expect to be shown the best and the nearest! Students sometimes refer ironically to the 'open day hall'!

Sarah

Went to a very useful university open day

'Mum took three of us in her car. I wasn't sure I wanted to go with a parent, but she said that we would split up when we got there. Anyway, my friends and I worked out how much it would have cost us to go by train! We had had to send in our names and give the subjects we were interested in in advance. When we got there we were all given programmes for the day, showing the times at which presentations on the different subjects would be given and listing other sessions we could attend as well. There was a separate programme for parents. Ours began with a welcome talk in a huge lecture hall and short talks from people like student services staff and the president of the Students' Union. The parents went off to have a welcome talk, followed by talks on topics the university thought parents would be more interested in – finance, loans, accommodation, careers and student life (that seemed to concentrate a lot on health and security – things like late-night buses). They were obviously out to convince parents that this would be a good environment to live in. They also heard about the different people students could turn to if they had problems. Mum then went to visit the medical centre and the careers service. We three split up and went to different departments then met up for lunch before joining one of the tours round the campus led by students, then did a hall visit. The hall was about three miles away, so we were taken by bus. We saw the dining room and common rooms, and could also look in two study bedrooms. They looked suspiciously tidy! We also had time to see the Students' Union building and walk round the campus by ourselves. The day was very good and I made that place one of the choices on my UCAS application.'

So, you can find out a lot by yourself. In addition, there are a lot of useful people you can ask for advice. Who?

People who you can ask for advice

Connexions personal adviser/careers advisers

You probably know who your adviser is and consulted him or her about your choices during year 11. They can tell you about employment and training in your area; about Apprenticeships, and the entry requirements for different careers. In their jobs they visit local employers to keep up to date with changes in the workplace, so they will be able to tell you not only which jobs are available but which companies are currently recruiting. When it comes to more detailed information on getting a job, they can help you with your application letter or form, tell you how to prepare a CV, and how to do well in job interviews. They can also help you with your decision if you decide on full-time higher education, and advise you on suitable courses – whether you want to find ones that will lead to a particular career, or whether you want to keep your options open for the time being. They can look with you at degree and Higher Diploma courses, and inform you about the entry requirements for different professions.

Do you want to know:

- which course you would need to do in order to qualify for a particular career, or set of careers?

- where a particular degree might lead?

- whether some careers that might interest you can be entered from degrees in *any* subject?

Then ask their advice.

They will also know which courses are 'qualifying' degrees to give you maximum exemptions from postgraduate training for certain professions like law and psychology, and which ones are not advisable if you might later want to teach.

They can often be helpful, too, with ideas for inclusion in your personal statement, particularly where vocational courses are concerned.

Careers teacher/guidance teacher

You will be having careers lessons – which may or may not include preparation for higher education. The careers teachers may know you quite well and have suggestions as to which direction might suit you. They will also provide assistance with job applications – probably through workshops in careers lessons. Topics like choosing higher education courses, applying through the different application systems, and preparation for higher education interviews, might be covered by other members of staff like your head of year or subject teachers.

Personal tutor/form teacher

They won't have the same expert knowledge as the careers specialists – but they will know you better as a person. They might also teach the subject that you hope to continue into higher education. It's a good idea to discuss choices and decisions with them too.

People working in the career you hope to enter

Will you be applying for a course that leads to a professional qualification and a specific career? If you can find someone already working in that career – ask their advice.

Warning – they can tell you about the job, but how long is it since they trained? Have they kept in touch with changes to courses? Then again, they may recruit or work with new entrants to the profession, so they could be bang up to date.

Your family

Parents, and older brothers and sisters know you too. You might think that your parents' information and ideas are out of date (and they might indeed be out of touch with current qualifications and entry requirements), but research shows that the majority of young people do listen to their parents when they are making career choices. If you have older brothers or sisters who applied for jobs or filled in higher education applications recently, they might be able to help with ideas and technical points (like looking through application letters and CVs, or personal statements on higher education application forms, and suggesting possible improvements). Then there are uncles, aunts and cousins. Don't forget them – if they happen to work in a relevant area.

Friends

And they also know you! They could be useful sources of advice as to whether you are right for a particular job or employer. Don't, though, fall into the trap of making joint decisions – for example, 'Let's all apply for a law degree, or for a job at Bloggs and Sons.'

Subject teachers

They can be very helpful if you are considering taking their subject in a higher education course. Sounds obvious, doesn't it? But, surprisingly, some students get as far as completing an application without consulting the person who has taught them for the last year.

Subject teachers:

- are familiar with the course content, teaching styles and methods of assessment in their subject at different universities and colleges. OK, it might be some time since they qualified, but they are probably in touch with past students from your school/college

- know you and your relative strengths and weaknesses in the subject. What's more they will be responsible for making your predicted grade. *If* a subject teacher advises you against doing that subject any further, think very hard.

Staff in universities and colleges

Students are sometimes afraid of making direct contact and asking questions. They think that they shouldn't be doing this – that they are applicants and they don't wish to appear difficult and prejudice their chances. Wrong! Staff are not monsters who will immediately put a black mark against your name if you dare to ask questions. A lot of them have teenage children themselves and know how difficult making choices can be. In any case, it's in their interests to recruit the right sorts of students. They are given retention targets, and if too many students drop out they are the ones to get the black mark! So, it is to their advantage to make sure that students get on to the right courses in the first place.

When you look at websites and prospectuses you will often see that a contact name and telephone number plus email address is given for the course. This may be the admissions tutor for the department – or often – the course leader. If you have any queries at all about a course that you are considering, contact them.

Current higher education students

Are there former students from your school or college at the institution you'd like to go to, or doing the course you want to do. Why not write to or email them? They are usually delighted to help – and you know the saying 'from the horse's mouth'?

(There is also a useful website, which contains details of the National Student Survey. More information on this in Chapter six.)

Students' Union

How about contacting the Students' Union at your intended places of study. They often produce their own (irreverent and brutally honest) guides to places.

Tips

There is so much to think about when choosing both a course and a place that it is easy to miss out on some of it. Here is a suggested list of steps to take.

Work out your priorities regarding subject, place, teaching methods etc.

- Look in the UCAS Directory – or use the website to find out which institutions offer the courses that interest you. Cross off all the ones that don't meet your requirements.

- Check the TQI website www.tqi.ac.uk

- Now you are ready to go to universities' and colleges' own websites.

- Read what is there – and cross off some more places!

- Now make a shortlist of places that really interest you, and get ready to do some in depth research.

This means doing the following.

- Reading their entry profiles on the UCAS website.

- Reading the QAA review reports.

- Sending for prospectuses and course leaflets.

- Going to a higher education fair, if there is one held near you.

- Visiting as many of the places on your now, hopefully, shorter shortlist as possible.

- If you can't get to an official open day, try to go there at another time and make your own visit. (You might not be able to talk to many people, but you can get a feel for the place – and for the nearest town or city. You might be able to go with friends who are also interested in the place – or persuade parents to take you one weekend.)

What now?

Is your head spinning yet?

The trouble with asking for advice is that most people are delighted to help and might blind you with information. The other problem is that you are bound to get conflicting advice (and possibly biased advice from some sources). The golden rule is to listen, question, discuss, then evaluate everything you have been told and make up your own mind. No-one else can do that for you. It's your life and your decision.

And if you get the decision wrong the first time it's not the end of the world. There are several references in this book to the fact that careers these days are flexible. That means, that if you think you've made a mistake or would be happier doing something else, there are ways round this throughout your working life.

Information

For information – as opposed to personal advice – you can get help from some very useful websites. Some are regional – so you will need to consult the one that is appropriate for you. More sources of information are given in Chapter eleven, but here is a shortlist of the sites to try.

Careers Scotland – www.careers-scotland.org.uk

Careers Wales – www.careerswales.com

National Connexions website – www.connexions.gov.uk

Connexions Direct website (for web chat or emailing an adviser) – www.connexions-direct.com

And your own Connexions company may have its own website too.

And when it comes to higher education courses, you can find some useful information on the UCAS website, www.ucas.com If you look there under 'Entry profiles' you will find that universities and colleges give details of their different courses under headings like:

■ entry requirements

■ methods of selecting students

■ personal characteristics students should possess in order to benefit from the course.

Unfortunately, not all institutions or courses have 'Entry profiles'. The number of those that do is increasing all the time, though.

Good and bad reasons for making a decision

Good

■ This course, job, training programme would really interest me.

■ I've weighed up the financial implications and am happy with them.

■ I know that full-time/part-time study is the way forward for me.

■ I have researched all the options and I'm sure that I have all the facts that I need.

Bad

■ I can't think what else to do – and I saw this job/course advertised.

■ The money's good.

■ My mother's, colleague's, sister's, friend's cat thinks that it would suit me.

■ Everyone says that this is a good employer/university.

■ It's what everyone else is going to do.

For a full list of useful addresses and websites, see Chapter eleven.

Chapter six
Choosing your higher education programme

There are 329 universities and colleges in the UCAS system (which organises applications to about 95% of all full-time higher education courses) and over 50,000 different courses!

You can see that there are a lot of choices to make before you put in a higher education application.

This chapter addresses four important questions:

- What will you study?

- How will you be taught and assessed?

- Where will you go?
- How will you choose?

What will you study?

Choosing a course is the first decision you have to make – and it won't be an easy one! You'll have seen just some of the subjects you could study given as examples in Chapter four. If you now look in the *UCAS Directory* (a paperback book, which should be in school or college) or on the UCAS website you'll see just how many there are.

Do you want to continue your favourite subject into higher education? Why not? It's what many people do and has the advantage that it will be familiar – at first that is. Doing this also has the benefit of giving you the opportunity to spend three or four years really going deeply into something you enjoy.

Even choosing known subjects needs care though. There is no rule that says that a subject or course with the same title at different higher education institutions must be the same. Far from it. Each university or college decides exactly what to include in the course content. A course in English, geography, economics… is *not* going to be the same wherever it is offered. So do check the course content carefully. Even if you think you know what you want, you will be surprised at the differences between courses. Take a subject like geography – it can be taught as an art or a science. Then there are variations on a theme. Did you know that you could study the following specialist biology courses:

- agricultural
- animal
- applied
- aquatic
- behavioural
- cell

- coastal marine
- computational
- conservation
- developmental
- environmental
- evolutionary
- field
- fisheries
- freshwater
- human
- imaging
- infection
- marine
- medical
- molecular
- plant
- quantitative
- social
- water
- wildlife?

Or that these courses could also interest someone taking biology:

- biodiversity
- biomechanics
- biomedical technology
- biophysics

- biotechnology

- coastal studies

- food

- genetics

- immunology

- life sciences

- microbiology

- neuroscience

- palaeobiology

- pathobiology

- psychobiology

- zoology?

There are, however, some common topics in most degree courses that have the same or similar titles. If you look at the Quality Assurance Agency (QAA) for Higher Education website, www.qaa.ac.uk/academicinfrastructure/programspec you will find that the typical content of just over 50 subjects is described there.

A new subject?

If you do not want to continue any of your present subjects there are literally dozens of subjects that can be started at degree or Diploma level. These range from hospitality management, ecology or planning through to Egyptology, linguistics or popular culture. Some can be started without prior knowledge; others will require an A level or equivalent knowledge of a related subject *or* will specify certain GCSE/S-grade passes.

Possible new subjects include:

- Chinese

- cognitive science

- conflict studies

- film studies

- financial services

- Hindu studies

- Islamic studies

- Latin American studies

- linguistics

- medicine

- museum studies

- journalism

- philosophy

- United States studies.

And there are many more – including some suggestions given in Chapter four.

Taking a completely new subject can be risky, unless you have really done your homework and found out what is involved. This brings us to:

Combined courses

If you want to keep options open for a while longer, there are hundreds of courses (known as either joint, combined or general courses) that allow you to take two or more subjects and specialise as your interests develop. This can be a good way of sampling an unknown subject. You can also, of course, do a combined course in familiar subjects too.

The options for combined courses are immense! You could choose to combine:

- totally new subjects – like history of art with Japanese

- two familiar ones – like maths and French

- one familiar one with one new one – for example German with film studies

- two general (or academic) – such as history and economics

- two vocational – like engineering with management

- one academic and one vocational – like geography with business studies

- two science subjects – like biology with chemistry

- two humanities or social science subjects – for example, sociology and English or religious studies with French

- one of each – like biology with history.

You can use www.ukcoursefinder.com to help to find the right subject.

Warning – if you are thinking of choosing a course that will lead towards a particular career you need to find out whether the content is sufficient to satisfy the requirements of professional bodies. This is another reason for careful checking of websites and prospectuses. Organisations like the Law Society, the Royal Institute of Chartered Surveyors, the General Medical Council and the British Psychological Society, oversee the activities of a particular profession and often accredit degree courses after examining the content. If you did an accredited degree you would be either qualified to practise the profession immediately, or would be exempted from some of the professional exams that have to be taken after a degree course in order to practise.

Does it matter which subjects you choose?

Yes, if you have a particular career in mind. If you want to work in the following career areas you will need to take a relevant course:

- agriculture and horticulture

- architecture

- construction

- dentistry

- engineering

- environmental protection

- medicine

- nursing

- professions related to medicine – physiotherapy, radiography etc

- public health

- science, including biology, chemistry, physics and specialisms based on these subjects, like geology, meteorology or pharmacy

- technology

- veterinary science

- and certain jobs in business and finance – such as actuary, economist, statistician – which require a degree in maths, economics or a closely related subject.

Many of the subjects on the preceding list form the first part of professional training for a career. For instance, a degree in architecture is the first part of training that includes supervised work experience and a vocational Diploma. Medicine, dentistry, the medically-related professions and veterinary science are fully integrated courses, in which theory, practice and clinical work are all combined in the degree course. Engineering is the first part of career training for most engineers. Although it is not strictly necessary to follow an engineering degree with approved professional training and study for a qualification known as Chartered Engineer, most engineering employers expect their graduate entrants to do so.

What may have surprised you is that certain subjects do not appear in the list. Would you have expected to find law, psychology, journalism, surveying, drama and social work there? They are excluded because although first degrees in these subjects do exist, they are not part of a compulsory route to qualifying. In some cases taking a degree would form a *quicker* route, but there are postgraduate routes available as well for people with degrees in *any* subject. There is, for instance, a one-year conversion course in law, which would add a year to your studies, but would also give you a free choice of degree subject. There are also postgraduate courses in social work, publishing, journalism, and town and country planning – to name just a few examples.

All this should be of some comfort if you have not yet made up your mind about a career. Most people, in fact, do not have clear career ideas when they begin their degree courses (unlike Diploma students who are normally studying in a vocational area). They decide what to do while they are on their courses – and many find that their interests and priorities change while they are students.

Where can other subjects lead?

There are dozens of careers open to students in any subject – and over two-thirds of jobs advertised for graduates do not specify a subject. What employers in these areas are looking for is a degree as a level of academic achievement – which shows that you are capable of learning quickly – and a range of personal qualities such as the ability to communicate, manage your time, or work in a team.

All of the following careers are open to graduates in any subject!

accountancy (chartered, certified, management & public sector)	administration	advertising (account executive or copywriter)
air traffic control	antique dealing	Army (officer level)
arts administration	auctioneering and valuing	banking (high street or investment)
bookselling	building society management	broadcasting (producer or programme assistant)
buying	charity fundraising	the Civil Service (including the Diplomatic Service)

computer programming	conference or events management	customs and revenue
estate agency	financial services	health service management
hotel management	housing	human resources (personnel)
immigration	IT	insurance (broking, claims assessing, underwriting)
journalism	law (barrister or solicitor)	leisure and recreation
librarianship	local government	logistics
loss adjusting	management consultancy	marketing
market research	Merchant Navy (officer level)	police
prison service	probation work	public relations
retailing	Royal Air Force	Royal Navy/Royal Marines
sales	social work	surveying
travel and tourism	youth work	web design

And there are more.

And the scientists, engineers and graduates from vocational courses can all do them too. (In fact too many engineers – for the sake of British industry that is – do!) They find that their skills are valued in more highly paid occupations such as investment analysis, investment banking and management consultancy, and head in those directions.

Have a look at the destinations of students from three different subjects. (Information given is from the publication *What Do Graduates Do?*, published by UCAS/CSU/AGCAS.)

Chemistry

From the latest figures available – of those graduates who entered employment as opposed to doing postgraduate study:

- only 40% entered chemistry and science related careers
- nearly 22% entered general management and administrative work
- nearly 8% went into financial work
- nearly 4% went into marketing, sales and advertising
- some entered the Armed Forces, the Police Force, health professions, the hospitality industry and public relations.

History

- over 40% were in general management and administrative work
- over 4% entered marketing, sales and retailing
- over 11% entered financial work
- 4% entered media and literary work
- some entered the Armed Forces, Police Force, retailing, the hospitality industry and health service.

Environmental studies/science and geography

- nearly 45% entered general management and administrative work
- 21% were in technical and scientific jobs
- nearly 4% went into marketing, sales and advertising
- over 12% entered financial work
- some entered the Armed Forces, the Police Force, librarianship, social work, the hospitality industry, the media and public relations.

What do employers want?

Why is it that so many careers – and employers offering them – do not specify particular degree subjects?

First, employers look for the skills that you should acquire while studying almost any subject. These are:

- analytical research
- clear presentation of ideas and projects
- logical reasoning and thinking
- organisation and time management
- problem solving.

However, not all of your time in higher education will be spent in the lecture room and the library. You will probably have a part-time job. You will want to have a social life as well – and through both of these you can also pick up some other skills that employers value. They are known as 'soft skills' and include:

Adaptability

Jobs are continually changing. After two years in a job, your tasks and responsibilities could be very different from your initial ones. You might have to retrain and will almost certainly need to update your skills and learn new ones. You can demonstrate that you are adaptable by doing things that students often enjoy doing, like travelling to different places in the holidays, or better still using part of the holidays (or of a gap year) to work on a paid or voluntary basis in a part of the country you have never been to before – or abroad.

Commercial awareness

Employers are always looking for ways to increase their income and decrease their costs. If they don't their businesses will not do very well and might even fail. You are almost certainly going to work in some pretty boring jobs while you are a student – to help with your budget. Even basic level jobs can reveal certain things. You might see examples of poor service. You might even have the chance to improve them.

Communication

You will have to communicate with the people you work with when you start on your career. You might also have to communicate with colleagues and customers. You might have to supervise junior staff. You will almost certainly have to produce written reports. You might have to explain things to people who do not understand as much about a topic as you do – but who would resent feeling patronised. During your course you should get the opportunity to give presentations. You could also practise communication in one of the typical part-time jobs that students do – in shops, bars or telephone call centres. If your university or college employs 'student ambassadors' who represent the institution at open days and higher education fairs you could gain communication experience by becoming one. Some ambassadors also visit schools to give talks.

Initiative

Most employers *don't* want people who simply do as they are told and keep the current system running smoothly. They want people with ideas who will make things happen. This is where taking part in organising a student club or other activity can help.

Leadership

Employers want people who could become managers. Again, taking the lead in a club, society or sports team can teach valuable leadership skills.

Numeracy

This can be tricky if you are going to do a humanities or social science course. But – if you can get a job in the Students' Union bar, in a local pub, or even in a fast food outlet where you have to take orders and give the correct change quickly, you will be able to prove that you have a basic level of numeracy.

Persuasive skills

This means getting people to do things by negotiating and persuading, rather than by barking out orders. If you share a flat or house during your time as a student you might have to do a lot of this – coaxing everyone into doing their fair share of the housework and cooking. If you go on holiday with a group of friends you might have to be diplomatic over choices to be made then.

Teamwork

You might, depending on the subject you choose to do, get some practice in this during the course. If not, you can add to your future employability by spending some of your free time playing in sports teams, taking part in voluntary work projects, joining an orchestra or choir…

Entry grades

These are important factors to take into account when choosing courses. You should not choose any course – Diploma or degree – without knowing that you are on course to meet the entrance requirements. It may seem unfair if your friend is asked for lower grades than you are – but this happens. It is easier to gain admission to some courses than others. Higher education is a marketplace. The grades and points asked for depend on the difficulty of the subject content, its popularity and the popularity of the university. Treat entry grades as a general guideline, but be realistic about your chances. With average grades you would be unlikely to get a place for veterinary science, whereas you should be able to get one somewhere for animal or equine science, although your choice of college may be restricted.

How will you be taught and assessed?

You might learn through a combination of lectures and discussion groups, or practical classes. Some places place more emphasis on formal lectures; others on work done in smaller groups – seminars and tutorials, or problem classes. These are all described in Chapter four. This is something to check before applying.

Another very important thing to check is the assessment methods. These vary widely. To give all the marks in final examinations at the end of the course is now not very common, but universities and colleges vary in the weighting they give to:

■ coursework

■ marks for selected assignments, essays, projects or dissertations

■ termly or yearly examinations.

If you can work under pressure in the exam room and prefer this method of assessment you are an exams person, and you might not like having to hand in pieces of coursework all the time. If you like to work steadily and can keep up with deadlines, you won't want to go to a place that gives you most of your marks for performance in examinations each term or semester.

Whatever the teaching and assessment methods, you'll find that you are given most of the responsibility for your own learning. It's up to you to turn up for classes, and it's up to you to do the work. No-one chases you. Of course, tutors are willing to help if you have any problems – but it's up to you to ask.

How three students chose their courses

Catt

Third-year student, BSc Hons business studies, currently doing a year's sandwich placement

'I wasn't very confident about my A level grades and nearly didn't apply for university. It was only when I went to see my Connexions adviser about possible jobs that I heard about foundation degrees. She didn't try to put me off employment, and in fact gave me the details of some very interesting sounding companies. She didn't try to influence me in any way, but stressed that it was my decision to make. (I almost wished she would tell me what to do!) However, I wrote down lots of points for and against each alternative on a sheet of paper – and eventually decided to apply for a foundation degree with the possible option of proceeding to honours if possible.

I was right about the A levels. I got Es in economics and maths and an N in English. I was right to choose the foundation degree too. I got very high marks and was able to move on to the honours degree. Those two years made a big difference to my confidence. I'm sure this was due to the extra support we were given. Most of the course was the same as the one followed by honours degree students, but we had additional workshops in small groups of ten.

I have now completed the first year of my honours degree course, which I chose because it offered a year's industrial placement. I felt that this would make me more employable. I work in a team, but we all have our individual projects to do. I'm based in the marketing department of a big pharmaceuticals manufacturer, working with full-time employees and have a supervisor who assigns my work and helps me if I have problems.'

Alex

Final-year student, BSc Hons physics

'I chose physics simply because it was the best grade I had in my Highers, and I also enjoyed it. I thought that it could lead to a good job, but I did know, though, that if I didn't want a career in physics afterwards I would be able to go into other jobs that would use my scientific mind and analytical skills. I thought about selling my soul to the City – or rather the financial services sector in Edinburgh, my home town for a while. A lot of young people work in banking and insurance there, and they all seem to have a good lifestyle. But now I have decided on a career in medical physics. Quite a change!'

Sunita

Second-year student, foundation degree in graphic design

'I have always been a creative sort of person, but it took me a long time to work out what I wanted to do. I had taken art, French, psychology and geography for AS, and art, psychology and geography for A2. Art was the one I enjoyed the most by a long way. First, I decided that I wanted to do a course in design of some kind and dithered between graphics, jewellery and then finally graphic. My art teacher agreed with this and promised me a good reference. My next decision was where to go. I didn't want to do a one-year art foundation course, so had to look through the UCAS book for places that didn't absolutely insist on one. My art teacher and head of year both advised me to do one – but I'm stubborn! I also wanted a place that would organise some good work experience for me, and I made another shortlist from those places that said in their prospectuses where they sent students.

My beautiful plans came unstuck when I wasn't offered one place! I found when I went for interviews that most other applicants had done foundation courses and that my portfolio wasn't good enough. But this university must have liked me and kept my application on file, because they wrote to me later to say that a new foundation degree was starting and offered me a place on it.

Towards the end of the year I did a two-week placement at a very small graphic design studio. There were only five staff, so I learned quite a lot about the business side as well as the creative one. They had to do their accounts and marketing and so on. It was the sort of firm I had always thought that I wanted to work in. This year I have done a second one with a large, advertising agency. I might change my mind now! I have almost decided to apply to transfer to the honours course in graphic design, but I'm going to try out the job market too.'

Where will you go?

Choosing a place

Deciding where to study is almost as important as deciding on a course. You are planning to spend several years in a place, so you need to be as sure as you possibly can be that you would be happy there. (That is where the importance of open days and visits comes in.) Everyone is different. Two students might go to the same institution for a day and come away with totally different reactions. One might appreciate the nearness of lecture rooms, halls of residence and social facilities on a small self-contained campus, while the other might have found it claustrophobic.

You will have a choice of the following.

- Large *civic* universities which are usually in major cities, like Manchester, Bristol or London. They can have more than 15,000 students and offer most subjects, including medicine. Academic buildings are in or near the city centre, possibly spread over several sites, but halls of residence are often on separate sites.

- Campus universities, originally on one site. They may have now outgrown that site or merged with other institutions like teacher training colleges or art schools, so that some departments and accommodation are on separate sites. They are often smaller than the civics but some campus universities are quite large. Note that there are some campuses in towns and cities. Birmingham, Nottingham and Reading are just three examples of universities that have most of their buildings in a parkland setting. Don't automatically assume that all city universities will be of the non-campus type.

- Universities that grew out of former polytechnics. They now offer a range of courses, but still have a slant towards vocational courses. They don't always offer subjects like history or English for example. They are often split sites.

- University sector colleges or institutes of higher education. There are not many of these left since they are rapidly obtaining university status! However, some still exist. Most originally specialised in one subject e.g. teacher training, or art and design. Most have expanded their range of courses or combined with other colleges, so now offer a wide range. They are generally smaller than most universities, although the biggest colleges are as large as the smallest universities.

■ Colleges of further (or of further and higher) education, which offer the majority of courses at level 3 or below, but also a significant number of higher education options. You are likely to find a number of Higher Diploma and foundation degree programmes in this sector – plus some degree courses. Many are now establishing links with higher education institutions, so that students can begin a foundation degree at a college and then move to university for the honours stage.

How will you choose?

Do you want to live in a big city like Leeds or London, with all the attractions (or distractions) of city life; or would you rather have a rural campus like Warwick, where your social life may be on site? Would you prefer to be a big fish in a small college like Lampeter (University of Wales) with less than 1500 students, or a small fish in a very large university like Nottingham with around 11,000 students, or Nottingham Trent with nearly 20,000? Do you want a strong college identity within a larger university like Cambridge, Durham, London or Oxford?

Again, everyone is different – but the following is a suggested list of questions to ask yourself.

■ Do I want to be in a large city, in a small town, or in the countryside? By the sea? By the mountains? (Important if your hobbies are sailing or climbing.) On a small campus outside an average size town? In a city centre?

■ How far away from home do I want to be? Somewhere where it's not too difficult to come home for weekends? Somewhere Mum and Dad can take me to each term? As far away as possible? In this case, do check how good access is by public transport –i.e. train or national coach service.

- Do I want to live at home? This option is becoming more popular given the rising cost of higher education. One drawback is that not every course is offered by every institution. If your nearest one doesn't offer the one you want, you might have to commute daily to one that does and that is within daily travelling distance.

- How important is the type of accommodation offered (and the cost)? How much is available and of which type? Do I want accommodation provided, if only for the first year? (Many students choose this option as a means of making the transition from life at home easier – and as a way of making friends. They then rent private accommodation with those friends in subsequent years.) Do I want to cook for myself or have meals provided? Do I want en suite facilities in my room? Would I prefer to live out and rent a flat or house with other people right from the start?

- How much will it cost me to live there apart from my rent and food? (See Chapter seven for more on this.) What does the website or prospectus have to say about annual expenditure? What would I have to pay in daily travel? What is the likely amount I might spend on social life?

- Does the university or college offer any bursaries that I could apply for?

- Does it cater for my special interests? You might want to be somewhere that has societies for musical activities, a strong amateur dramatic club, an officer cadet corps, a particular sport etc.

- Does the course offer work experience – or the possibility of sponsorship?

- Could I spend part of my course in another country?

- How easy is it to find term-time jobs nearby?

How else might you choose a place?

By looking at *student destinations* perhaps?

People sometimes look at the jobs entered by students from a particular institution. If they got good jobs you should do so too? Right? Surely this will be a reliable factor?

Well, yes and no. University departments are required to publish information on student destinations. However, do read beyond the '93% employment' bit. Are the graduates working in blue chip companies or in 'McBurger' jobs? Consult prospectuses and websites for examples of employers who have recruited their students. If the information is not there – ask for it. A department should know what its last year's graduates are doing. Although, to be fair, the information isn't always easy to come by. A lot of students are reluctant to complete questionnaires – or simply forget to do so. It depends also at what time the surveys were done. A huge number of students, asked to give details of their jobs in the first few months after leaving higher education, would give information on the temporary jobs they are doing to pay off debts and keep body and soul together while looking for a 'proper' job.

Even the information published in *What do graduates do?* (quoted elsewhere in this chapter) doesn't give the whole picture. This annual publication uses data collected by the national 'Destination of Leavers from Higher Education' survey, which includes data supplied by students from all higher education institutions. There is an employment category 'Retail assistants, catering, waiting and bar staff', which has a suspiciously high number of students from most subjects. But this survey is done in January every year and is based on students who graduated in the previous June. Six months on, many are more than likely to be still in temporary jobs. A category 'Clerical and secretarial occupations' also contains high numbers, which again might reflect the numbers not yet in settled long-term work.

What about the *reputation* of a place?

Aha, now you can look at league tables published in the national press, can't you? Well – the best advice is to take these with a large pinch of salt. Which criteria do they use? Degree results? Employment rates? What else?

Have you read more than one quality newspaper's tables? If so, were institutions always given the same ranking? No, is the probable answer – and you need to know why. One paper compares universities across 49 subjects, concentrating mainly on the quality of their teaching. Another ranks 93 universities according to outcome of teaching assessments. A third ranks 101 universities offering a full range of subjects (i.e. not specialist institutions) and uses nine factors to construct the ranking. *The Times Higher Education Supplement* is the only one to include colleges. So you do need to know first which criteria are used in the survey you are looking at. Second, you need to know whether they are the same ones that are important to you!

Nevertheless, there is an established hierarchy. No-one can deny that some universities have more status than others. The pecking order is 'old', research-led universities (particularly the 19 which refer to themselves as the Russell Group), followed by new universities (the former polytechnics), then colleges. Some major employers do indeed recruit mainly from the first group. *But* beware! Some respected institutions don't teach some subjects as well as some of their newer competitors – the employers who do want particular subjects are well aware of this. Then, too, the status and reputation of a subject at university A can change if the members of staff who gave it that reputation move to university B!

Official surveys

There are actually some of these!

The Quality Assurance Agency for Higher Education (QAA) monitors the standard of education in higher education institutions. Universities and some colleges are responsible for the standards of their own courses and are able to award their own degrees. Some, usually smaller, colleges have to make an arrangement with a degree-awarding university to validate their programmes. The QAA conducts external quality assurance, which examines how well the universities are monitoring their standards. You can read QAA reports on the internet at www.qaa.ac.uk/reviews They contain the survey teams' conclusions on the reliability of the information each institution produces on its:

- standards

- quality of teaching

- and the information it produces on courses.

You can search either by subject or by university/college.

A teaching quality information website has been launched: www.tqi.ac.uk It carries reports and statistics on the quality of teaching in all universities and higher education colleges in the UK. Students' opinions will be represented since the results of a new National Student Survey, conducted in England, Northern Ireland and Wales, asking students what they think of the quality of their courses will be included on this site.

How they chose where to go

Anil

Second-year student, medicine

'My choice of places was limited by the subject I had chosen. Only a certain number of universities have medical schools. This was an advantage actually. I had a smaller number of prospectuses to read, unlike a mate applying for maths who looked at just about every university in the country. I come from Birmingham so I'm a city person – and luckily, I wouldn't like a rural campus. I ruled out a couple of medicine courses that had just started up in smaller towns, and basically concentrated on cities in the Midlands and the north. I don't think that there are many big cities in the south. I didn't have to look too closely at the content of the different courses either. They do have differences and varying electives that you can take – but, essentially, they are training you to be a doctor and must include a lot of the same topics.

This place is cool. There is a huge student population, loads of cheap places to eat near the student village where I share a flat – and the city centre has everything – shopping centres and squares with all the major chains, plenty of restaurants and very, very good clubs and good night life.'

Michelle

Final-year student, BA Hons media studies, at a university college in a small cathedral city

'Coming from the Isle of Man, where there are no big towns, I'd feel out of place in a large city. My home town has a community feel and you can get to know lots of people. I chose my subject early on, but finding a place to do it was more difficult. Media studies is done in a lot of places, but I ruled out most of the universities because they were so large. Most of the suitable places were colleges of higher education or university colleges. I didn't know what they were so I looked up several of their websites. Then I chose this one and was very pleased when they accepted me.

This college is very friendly. It's easy to get to know people – which was good when I was a bit homesick at first. I became involved in the Students' Union early on, and found it a great way to meet students from other years and courses. Before I arrived I thought that I'd have to go to the nearest large town for social life. It's mentioned quite often in this college's prospectus, but I've only been a few times. This is a small place, but there are pubs the students use. (I work part-time in one of them.) Then so much goes on at the Union. My life really revolves round that, and I am now on the entertainments committee. We put something on every night – music, karaoke, live bands, and do cheap drink offers. We try to offer a varied entertainments schedule throughout the year, in order to involve first years who might be sitting in their rooms feeling lost – but also students from all years.'

Hywel

First-year student, foundation degree in engineering

'My course leads to a degree from my nearest university, but is run jointly by the university and the further education college where I did my National Diploma. This year I am at the college and I'll spend the second year at the university. I chose to do this because my family wanted me to stay at home – they can't afford to give me much money – and also because I wouldn't have to make such a big change. The work is much more advanced, but I'm not having to get used to new surroundings and new people. Several of my friends from last year are doing the same course. The course is brilliant. I'm enjoying all the theory, since I can see how it relates to work. I am just completing my first project – on mass production. It involves a lot of the things we have covered in lectures on autocad, maths and electronic principles. In pairs, we have to design a barbecue incinerator for a garden. We are each taking certain aspects. We will combine them into a final design on the CAD system and make a joint presentation to the class. The next one will be on a one-off production theme.

I am expected to do a lot of my own research – looking things up and reading around the subject in the library. The staff are preparing us for next year at the university when we will have much more responsibility for managing our time. They are also giving us sessions on how to take our own notes, and how to use sources of information. By then, I shall be ready for the transfer, and I'm looking forward now to being at a bigger place, meeting new people and enjoying some of the social facilities there.

When I have completed the foundation degree I am definitely going to stay on and convert it into a full degree.'

Chapter seven
Financing higher education

It's true that doing a higher education course costs money. The days that your parents remember, when higher education was free and there were grants to cover living costs, have long gone. Yes – you really could get a degree at no cost and leave university with just a small overdraft or no debt at all! Now, even if you were eligible for all the financial assistance available, you would not be able to cover the cost of doing a full-time course. There are sources of help available, though, and it is well worth finding out what they are before you do your sums.

The press is full of horror stories about students graduating with huge debts to pay off. Barclays' annual survey, in 2005, estimated that the average student in England and Wales was leaving higher education before the introduction of higher tuition fees, owing £13,501. (See page 19 in Chapter two for the Government's estimate for future students.) But that's an average. Not every student leaves with the same size of debt. Some are fortunate enough to receive financial help from their parents and do not need to borrow as much as others. Some are more careful and manage their money better than others.

What is the likely cost?

That is very difficult to answer. A lot depends on where you choose to study. Some towns and cities are much more expensive than others to live in – so this naturally affects the amount of rent you'll have to pay for accommodation. You can't escape tuition fees, although they too can vary. Then there is your individual lifestyle to consider. Are you a party animal or a stay in with a good book/television programme person? All these variables explain why different universities and colleges estimate the cost of living there, *excluding tuition fees*, as being from £5000 to £15,000!

Looking at costs, let's start with tuition fees. These are fixed by other people. You can't do anything to cut them (unlike your social life expenses) but you can make sure that you get all the help that you are entitled to. You will have to pay up to £3000 a year in tuition fees at a publicly funded university or college in England or Northern Ireland. This excludes establishments like some performing arts colleges and a small number of other private institutions, which charge higher fees. Publicly-funded institutions are allowed to set their own fees, up to this maximum figure of £3000. All but four of the English universities have decided to charge this amount for all their courses. But not all students will pay the full amount.

Incidentally, whereas you will have to pay living costs up front, tuition fees can be paid *after* you graduate. You may pay them in advance if you are able to and wish to do so, but you will be allowed to apply for a low-interest loan from the Student Loans Company, which is owned by the Government. You can apply for the exact amount of the cost of the tuition fee, and the Student Loans Company will pay the money direct to the higher education institution. You will not have to pay back the loan until after you have left and are earning at least £15,000 a year. Interest payable on the loans is related to inflation, so that what you repay will, at the time you repay it, be about the same as what you borrowed.

However, *where* you live in the United Kingdom can also affect the level of tuition fees you will be charged, as follows.

■ The Welsh Assembly has stated that it will not permit Welsh institutions to charge variable fees until the academic year 2007/2008. The fixed fee for 2006/7 will be £1200. *But, students who start courses in 2006 will have to pay the larger fee from 2007 onwards.*

■ And, if you will be resident in Scotland *and* attending a Scottish institution, instead of paying tuition fees you will pay a graduate endowment at the end of your course – a one-off payment, currently £2154 (but set to rise by a small amount each year with inflation).

So, tuition is one expense. What else will you have to budget for? Books, equipment, visits, and unless you live at home, food and accommodation. The last two, plus expenditure on going out and general social life are the biggest – and also the most variable.

Accommodation costs

Accommodation costs vary according to whether or not meals are provided and the level of facility you require. Prices also vary according to area, with London and other major cities usually being more expensive. For example, at one end of the scale you could choose a single room with en suite facilities, at the other a shared room with a bathroom along the corridor. Some halls charge students a lower rent because they are some distance from the main university campus. This is balanced by the fact that you will have to pay daily bus fares.

So, accommodation costs could be around, say, £3000-£4000 per year.

The table below shows the different rates for accommodation at a large university college in the Midlands, according to the level chosen.

Type	37 weeks	42 weeks	43 weeks
En suite, on campus	£2516	£2856	£2924
En suite, off campus	£2146	£2436	£2494
Not en suite, on campus	£1776	£2016	£2064

All of the prices listed are for self-catering accommodation.

In London, one institution offers self-catering single rooms without private facilities for £112 per week.

What about books and equipment?

You can cut down here by using the well known trick of not buying every book on your reading list. Use library copies where you can, share some with friends, and buy only the most essential books for each subject. Field trips and visits will add up (and art students will have to pay for materials).

So, books might cost you, say, £300-£400.

Social life?

That's up to you! To give you some idea of likely costs for one year in higher education you can usually get an estimated figure by looking at university or college websites.

From a university in the north of England

Here is one estimate from a university in a large city in the north of England (which rates itself one of the cheapest for students to live in). The figure is for rent, food, energy, books, clothing, travel and entertainment. The two different estimates are useful because if – as many students do – you choose to share a house or flat in the private sector with other students, you will probably be expected to pay rent for the full year. Many students now stay in their university or college accommodation during part of the vacations.

Academic year only	£6600
Full calendar year	£8700
The total for the *academic year* breaks down like this:	
Self-catering accommodation for academic year	£2750
Food (£33 a week)	£1520
Gas and electricity	£280
Laundry	£200
Books and equipment	£350
Misc. e.g. travel, entertainment, TV licence, insurance	£1500
Total	**£6600**

At this particular university accommodation costs vary depending on facilities, the distance from the campus, and whether you share a room. Self-catering accommodation rents vary between £1250 and £3450. In halls of residence the costs are between £2000 and £3700 per academic year – but as meals are included in this, you would need to spend less on food (but should budget some money for extras, snacks and some meals out).

From a university in the South West

Expenditure	52 weeks
Rent (£50-£90, average £76 per week)	£3952
Food (£30 per week)	£1560
Books, materials and equipment	£250
Personal toiletries	£208
Laundry and housekeeping	£208
Clothes	£364
Local travel	£260
Leisure/social (£18 per week)	£936
TV licence	£116
Contents insurance (£3000 belongings and £1000 computer)	£70
Total	**£7924**

From a university in a Scottish city

Expenditure	Per week
University halls of residence, standard room with most meals	£120
Weekday lunches	£18
Laundry, toiletries, postage, insurance, telephones, clothes, limited entertainment	£35
Local travel	£10
Total	**£183**

(In self-catering accommodation students can expect to pay around £80 per week for rent, £55 for food, £8 for bills (fuel etc), £35 for personal expenditure and £10 for travel. This make a total of £188.)

Students will also need a minimum of £250 each year, for textbooks and basic stationery.

Institutions point out that these figures are only estimates – and that many students live on less.

Two students

The careful

'I rent a house with three friends for £50 a week each, plus another £10 a month for gas and electricity. We each spend about £60 a month on food and household stuff at a supermarket, and buy some fruit and vegetables at the local market. We mostly cook and eat together, but do eat out locally too. The area where we live is very student friendly. Pubs and clubs do midweek promotions.

My weekly expenditure varies, because when I am on clinical placement I might have to spend £10 a week on fares. I usually buy a new pair of shoes, at £25, for each placement too, since they wear out so quickly.

When I am at the university an average week might look like this:

Monday

■ walk to lectures – so no fares

■ £3.50 for a sandwich and soft drink at lunchtime

■ cook supper together from food stock.

Tuesday

■ similar to Monday

■ eat in again and rent a video.

Wednesday

- a half-day – so make and eat lunch at home
- cook again in the evening too
- then go out to a pub – it's promotion night, drinks are £1, so say £5 for the evening.

Thursday

- university all day again
- take homemade sandwich to save money
- but – fed up of cooking so we go out in the evening (there's a pub near us that does '248b48' – two main meals for £8 if you order before 8pm).

Friday

- university all day
- I work on Friday evenings in a club – so a quick and easy supper – maybe a pizza
- free security bus home.

Saturday

- up late after last night
- go into town to look at shops
- look is all that I do – although when I do need clothes there are lots of places selling four tops for £15
- either eat in followed by a club *or* do another evening shift at the one I work in.

Sunday

- meet up with friends in a pub
- real prices now – £3.20 a drink!
- might eat too.

Averaged out, I probably spend £40-£50 a week on eating out and socialising. A Saturday night in a club costs £30, so a week including one of those pushes up the total. (Midweek it's £15-£20.)'

(This student had no fees to pay as she receives an NHS bursary.)

And another...

'I started my first year with savings of £2000. I ended it over £2000 in debt. How could that happen? I had some heavy expenses – but even so I managed more badly than any of my friends. Money just disappeared in the first week! I had to pay a term's rent – and accommodation was particularly expensive. My self catering hall cost £3000 for the year. I also had tuition fees to pay (£1100) and books to buy. But I also made lots of mistakes afterwards. I was a typical student, I suppose. I felt rich with my savings and my loan. I also had accounts with two banks. I drew out whatever I needed, lived on microwave meals and went out a lot. Social life was awesome. I went out almost every night for a while. There was a free bus to take to us into the town centre, where clubs are good. But I ended up paying for taxis home. Drinks at £1.00 or £1.50 sound like a bargain, but when you add them all up... I also spent £30-£40 a month on my mobile phone.

One bank got rather nasty about my overdraft. My father paid that off, but I now have to work over the summer just to repay him and the other bank.

I don't want to be the equivalent of £4000 down next year – but I have plans! I'm moving into a shared house at a much lower rent. We are going to take it in turns to cook, and I'm aiming to restrict myself to spending £30 a week on social life.

My advice to new students is: money can just slip through your fingers, don't buy anything you don't really need, cut down on night life *and* don't use credit cards.'

(This student's expenses did not include the higher rate tuition fees.)

Financial assistance

There is government assistance, in the form of loans and grants – and you might be able to claim more than you think. There are also other sources of income to explore. The following outlines the possibilities.

Student loans

There are actually two loans available. One is the **fee deferment loan,** mentioned earlier. The second loan is the **maintenance loan.** In addition to the loan to pay your tuition fees, you can apply for another low-interest loan from the Students Loan Company to help with living and studying expenses. All students can receive 75% of the maximum loan. Whether you can get any or all of the remaining 25% depends on your income and that of your household (i.e. your parents' combined yearly income). Loans are payable in three instalments – one at the start of each term. Again, you will not have to pay back either loan until you have left university and are earning at least £15,000 a year, and then at a rate linked to your income. Repayment of both loans is made by automatic deductions from your salary, made by your employer.

The maximum amount that a student may borrow is fixed for the start of each new academic year. For the academic year 2006/07, the maximum loan for students studying in London will be £6170. For students studying in other cities it will be £4405. Loans are also available to students who choose to live at home, and they will be entitled to borrow up to £3415. 'Up to' means that the amounts available are based on family income. The maximum amount is not automatic. In order to arrange a loan you will have to complete an application form giving details of family income. You will then be informed how much you may borrow. However, you should be aware that the maintenance loan entitlement for maintenance grant recipients (see below) will be reduced by up to £1200 (as up to £1200 of the maintenance grant is paid in substitution for part of the loan).

Note – you will not receive any money during the summer vacation. Your student loan effectively has to last for the whole year. If you are unable to find a job over the summer or your parents are unable to support you, you will have to budget for rent, food, travel, social life, clothes and everything else. Some students do try to save from their loan to cover the summer period, but in reality this is not usually possible. If you do find a job over the summer you have more money per week to cover all your other expenditure during the academic year.

Scottish students receive smaller loans as they do not pay tuition fees.

Maintenance grants

From 2006/07, new student maintenance grants will be available. If your family income is £17,500 or less, you are likely to be eligible for the full maintenance grant from the Government, worth £2700. Partial grants on a sliding scale are offered to those with a household income of between £17,501 and £37,425 (2006/07 figures). Maintenance grants will be paid in three instalments – one at the start of each new term. Your local education authority will assess whether you are eligible for a grant. (The Government says that it expects 50% of all students to receive *some* support.) N.B. As mentioned above, up to £1200 of the grant will be paid in substitution for part of the student maintenance loan.

Bursaries

Universities and colleges that decide to charge the full £3000 fee must automatically award bursaries to students whose family income is below a certain level. Higher education institutions have announced different figures – so you might want to do a search! All must offer at least £300 to students who are eligible for the full £2700 maintenance grant. Some are offering £500, £800, £1000… to students on certain income levels. Some offer a package of benefits as, for example, the one offered by the university shown below.

For students entitled to the maximum maintenance grant

'In addition to the £300 bursary, we will also offer you a further bursary of either £1000, or a package of goods and services designed to help you settle into university life in your first year. This package is equivalent in value to £1200 and includes:

- loan of a laptop computer, with an option to purchase at the end of the course (estimated value £650)

- £200 reduction in the first term's university accommodation

- a local bus pass for the first term (current value £100)

- a sum credited to the catering service for the purchase of meals (value £50)

- a university print card (value £50)

- a sum credited to the university bookshop account (value £50)

- a further sum to be used at your discretion for a university sports card (current value £45), credit towards services offered by the Students' Union, or additional purchases from the university bookshop (value £100).'

All this is very complicated and the figures may have changed before you read this, so please check on the websites listed in Chapter eleven, and also each individual university or college website – where you should find information on their own support packages.

Bank loans

Bank loans or, more likely, free overdrafts up to a certain sum are another income source. The major banks are keen to attract student customers. They want to be able to keep you once you start earning. Overdrafts are usually free up to an agreed limit – but beware of high penalty charges if you accidentally (or otherwise) go over it!

Charitable trusts

They may make small payments to students on certain courses, living in certain geographical areas, or whose parents are/were employed in particular industries. The amounts, though, are usually small – and applications for assistance far exceed the money available.

Parents

The Government always assumes that parents will help to pay for your higher education. This is reflected in the fact that the amount you may borrow in student loans is decided on their income. Many parents do help of course. But some are unable to provide cash to help you out – or unwilling to do so. If you don't receive any financial support from them you can't claim any more from the Government. Financial help from parents can come in many forms, however. If you go home for the vacations you might live rent free and be fed. If you live at home throughout the course you will be living either free of charge, or much more cheaply than if you were paying accommodation costs somewhere else.

Scholarships

It is always worth checking on websites and in prospectuses to see whether universities and colleges offer any of these. The number is increasing – and there are varying kinds. Some for instance are given to students with excellent entry grades; others as the result of an essay competition. They rarely have strings attached but the sum of money is usually smaller than that of a sponsorship or bursary. Others are linked to high level skill in sport or music and these normally do have conditions attached to them – such as a requirement for students to sing in the university or local cathederal choir, play the college organ at services, or to be a member of a sports team.

Some scholarships are awarded for the entire length of the course; others for the first year only.

Sponsorship

How does sponsorship work? It is an arrangement between students taking certain subjects and employers who hope to recruit them when they graduate. In return for a sum of money you would work at their premises during some of your vacations, and should be interested in a permanent job with them. (You might or might not be offered a job at the end of the sponsorship period depending on the company's financial situation and your mutual satisfaction with each other.) Sponsorship money can definitely be useful. Amounts vary, with the average being about £1500 per year. You might, however, have to apply to courses from a list approved by your sponsor – which could limit your choice of university. Also, your summer vacations would be shortened.

Some sponsorships are available all through the course – and you would apply for one of these at the same time as completing your higher education application. Many sponsors, though, prefer to establish links with university departments and choose students who are already on certain courses. They know what they are getting that way! In other words, they know what students have learned to date, and what they are capable of doing work-wise. You could check whether the universities you are considering have any such arrangements.

Your own earnings

Most students now work for around 12-15 hours a week in term time. You are not really supposed to go over this officially as your academic work might be affected. But the attitude of universities and colleges to part-time work in term time has changed radically. Once it was definitely frowned on, if not forbidden. However, reality has set in. First, it is accepted that all but the richest students need to work in order to survive financially – and second, there is a realisation that employers actually prefer applicants who have work experience, even in menial jobs. (They find them more realistic and with skills in communication and commercial awareness that they have gained from working.)

At many higher education institutions you will find that some jobs around the campus (cleaning, office work, catering) are reserved for students, and that the Students' Union employs students in its bars and shops! But many universities and colleges go further than this by running **job shops,** which help to find part-time work that fits in with students' free time and cover all sorts of work from the usual bar and shop work, to work in customer services, call centres and help desks, or even to administrative and scientific jobs that are related to degree coursework. The better ones also negotiate reasonable wages and safe transport home after late night working.

Extra help for certain courses

Courses in health professions

If you study audiology, chiropody, dental hygiene, dental therapy, dietetics, midwifery, nursing, occupational therapy, operating department practice, orthoptics, physiotherapy, prosthetics and orthotics, radiography and speech therapy – and have an NHS funded place – you will qualify for an NHS bursary. This means that you will get free tuition, and can also apply for a means-tested bursary. Nor will you pay fees after the fourth year of a degree in medicine or dentistry. Nursing *Diplomas* are funded differently. Students on these courses get free tuition plus non means-tested bursaries of over £5000. (For this reason some universities recommend doing the Diploma then a degree top up.)

Dance and drama

Other sources of finance include **Dance and Drama Awards**, which are available for students attending practical courses (leading to National Diplomas and National Certificates) at certain private institutions. For more information see: www.dfes.gov.uk/financialhelp/dancedrama

Extra help for certain students

If you have disabilities you may qualify for extra grants (which do not have to be repaid) to cover expenses such as specialist equipment or personal helpers. You can get more information on this from Skill, the National Bureau for Students with Disabilities.

If you are leaving care, there is a small weekly grant that you can claim to help you with living costs over the summer vacations. Your social worker will have the details. Information is also available at www.doh.gov.uk/surviveoutthere/index.htm

Part-time students

Unfortunately, if you decide to take a higher education course on a part-time basis, including study through the Open University, you will have to pay your tuition fees up front and will not be eligible for a student loan. (Fees vary from institution to institution, and will be a proportion of the full-time costs.)

The assumption here on the part of the Government is that part-time students are in employment and can afford to pay, and that in many cases their employers will be paying fees for them. This is likely to be true if you are in full-time employment and being given day release by an employer; possibly so if you attend evening classes. If you decide to get part-time work as a way of funding your higher education, though, you could slip through the net of student support.

But you might be able to apply for some support *if* you get the proportion of work and study right. Part-time students have to be studying for 50% of an equivalent full-time course before they become eligible for official Government support. If you do qualify there are three different rates of means-tested grant available, depending on the number of hours you spend each week on a course and on your family income. You might also be able to get a grant of up to £250 to help with travel, books and other costs.

FAQs

As a student will I have to pay council tax?

Students are exempt from paying this tax, so there should be no problem if you live in a hall of residence or share private accommodation with other students. If you shared with one (non-student) adult, they could still claim the 25% single occupancy discount. If there are two or more other adults in the property the full tax is payable.

Suppose I decide to try to manage without a loan for my tuition fees – do any universities and colleges allow you to pay in instalments and how do I find out?

The decision to do so is entirely at the discretion of individual universities and colleges. Some do allow termly, as opposed to annual, payments. The only way to find out will be to ask them directly. If neither the prospectus nor the website gives the information, ring or email to ask.

At what rate do I pay back my student loan?

When your salary reaches the figure of £15,000 you will have to pay it back in monthly repayments of 9% of your income each year over £15,000. So at a salary of £16,000, your repayments would be £7 a month, at £20,000 your repayments would be £37 and at £25,000, £75. The loan is often quoted as being interest free, but is in fact at a low rate of interest as the amount is linked to inflation. So you will repay more than you borrowed.

Chapter eight
Taking a gap year

Gap years began – and were taken by a small number of pre-university students only – when it was common to stay at school for an extra term after A levels in order to prepare for and take the entrance examination for Oxford and Cambridge. Students were left with time to kill from approximately January to October. Several took off overseas on various forms of organised voluntary work. Now, increasing numbers of students take a gap year, or time out, between leaving school and starting in higher education. But the term has widened – as have the numbers and backgrounds of the 'gappers'. 'Gap' no longer means simply spending time overseas whether working or backpacking. Some students do voluntary work – overseas or at home; some travel; and others need the year for work in any jobs they can find so that they can save to help pay for their higher education costs. Some do a mix of things in their gap year, including any of travel, paid work, voluntary work and study. (Some go abroad to learn a language, or take an IT or secretarial skills course.)

Gap years (which, strictly speaking, are more like 15 months from the end of A levels, or Highers, to the beginning of your first term in higher education) could come in many shapes and forms and do not have to cost the earth – although some options cost more than others. Gap years are not solely for the last minute decision takers – although some students do decide to take a year out after getting their exam results. It's far preferable, as many do, to decide in advance, apply for what is known as deferred entry to higher education (which means that you apply, may be interviewed, and are offered conditional places just like all other applicants – but for the following year.) They are not just for the rich either. Although Prince William famously spent part of his gap year cleaning toilets while doing voluntary work in South America, he and other volunteers on the project had been expected to raise part of the money towards their costs through sponsorship or organising fundraising activities. OK so Dad probably forked out for the rest of the year…

The arguments against

Are there any drawbacks to taking a gap year? If this thought doesn't pass through your mind it will almost certainly interest your parents. The first question they usually ask is 'Do higher education institutions look favourably on gap years or disapprove?' Answer – most approve – and say so in their prospectuses. They find that ex-gap-year students are more mature, better able to handle their finances and stand on their own feet, while those who have travelled or lived away from home are less likely to become homesick. Others approve on the whole, but leave the decision to individual subject departments and advise you to check their policy. You might find that the occasional maths or physics admissions tutor, for instance, would prefer you to take a gap year after getting your degree. They argue that their subjects are best studied continuously with no break in work patterns. But many are fine with the idea.

A second argument against taking a break is that you might lose all motivation for higher education in the year. If that is so, the motivation probably is not very strong! You might not be ready for higher education at all!

What about eventual employers? The good news here is that employers of graduates are usually very enthusiastic. They appreciate the extra maturity too – but also the evidence of initiative, organisational ability and receptiveness to new ideas and experiences. And as far as voluntary work is concerned, recent research by Community Service Volunteers shows that 79% of members from the Association of Graduate Recruiters agreed that graduates who possessed skills gained through volunteering progressed through a work organisation more quickly.

Having something different on your CV can also make you stand out among applicants for a job, and if you have had a gap year you are likely to be asked about it and what you gained from it. *This will be most important.* Anyone can go on an organised expedition or holiday. Not everyone will have visited out-of-the-way places independently, or done some of the more interesting and out-of-the-way projects. The trick – just like talking about your out-of-school activities at an interview for a job or higher education place – is to be able to identify skills that you gained in the gap year, or to explain how you were changed by the experience.

So what kind of gap year might interest you?

You can think about any of the following ways of spending it.

Voluntary work in the UK

If you can't afford to travel, but would like to do something to help other people – and gain some skills at the same time that might be relevant to a future job or course application – you could think about contacting organisations that place volunteers on short-term projects in the UK. There are dozens, and you will find them listed on some of the gap-year websites, and in some of the books recommended in Chapter eleven. One of the best known is Community Service Volunteers (CSV), which places young people (and others) to work with children with special needs, drug and alcohol users, refugees, young offenders, homeless adults and disabled people. Volunteers commit to spending between 4 and 12 months on community projects. They receive free accommodation, food and travel expenses, plus a weekly living allowance. The current weekly allowance is £45. See www.csv.org.uk for more information.

You could also work with organisations such as:

■ the British Trust for Conservation Volunteers, which organises working holidays and projects lasting from a minimum of three months – useful experience for students applying to environmental studies or science courses (www.btcv.org)

■ the National Trust, which can place volunteers in different aspects of its work for periods from three months to one year (www. nationaltrust.org.uk/volunteering)

■ the Corrymeela Community, a Christian organisation which is committed to the work of reconciliation in Northern Ireland and beyond

■ the Independent Living Foundation whose volunteers help people with severe disabilities to remain in their own homes by providing personal care – volunteers are paid a wage and given free accommodation (usually in London)

■ the Simon Community which runs night shelters and residential houses for homeless people – volunteers go out to make contact with people sleeping rough.

And there are many more. Such types of work would give you valuable experience for training courses and work in social work, teaching, youth work, the Police Force and careers related to medicine in which social and communication skills are important.

Voluntary work overseas

Perfectly possible – but this one will almost invariably require you to raise some money towards the cost of the project. Examples of projects include:

- teaching a school subject in developing countries

- working as a sports coach

- teaching English in China, Ghana, India, Mexico, Nepal, Peru, Thailand, Togo or the Ukraine

- working on a kibbutz

- caring for children in a Romanian orphanage

- working in residential homes with elderly people or people with disabilities

- working on environmental and conservation projects

- building classrooms in a rural African village.

Lots of organisations need energetic and enthusiastic volunteers. You are bound to find something to suit your particular interest, whether this is in environmental projects or in social or medical work. The drawback to these projects is that most organisations expect volunteers to raise a certain sum of money towards the cost of the project. If you want to go for a whole year these can mount up, but shorter periods are possible. Two of the most experienced are GAP and Project Trust which send hundreds of young people abroad every year. (They do provide successful applicants with fund-raising ideas – and say, incidentally, that the students they select *never* have any difficulty in raising the money.) The advantage of going on an organised project is that you will be looked after in any kind of difficulty, and will have proper insurance arranged for you. However, organisations should be carefully checked out. Some have proved to be not quite so good at arranging placements as they claimed to be, and there have been letters of complaint from parents on this subject in the national press. The **Year Out Group** is worth a look, since it is supported by the Department for Education and Skills, so the agencies it lists are reputable.

Voluntary work in Europe

Lots of organisations help students to organise voluntary work placements in Europe. However, there is also a programme funded by the European Commission, the European Voluntary Service programme, which enables young people aged between 18 and 25 to work in another European country. Volunteers work on projects that last between six and twelve months. Under this scheme you could participate in environmental projects, theatre or arts projects with minority groups, or work with children or elderly people.

Paid work in the UK

You know all about finding jobs in this country. You probably have one already. But there are more interesting (and better paid) things to do than serve or deliver pizza. Some of the ideas in that follow would pay you a wage. (Others would cost you money…)

A learning experience

There are paid positions you could take that would give you experience and something to write on the UCAS or job application form, such as:

- salaried positions as care assistants – for anyone eventually hoping to enter the medical professions

- the Year in Industry (YINI) scheme, which places more than 800 students each year with companies that give them real hands-on work. Some of the companies are very well known. You would be paid a reasonable salary, be given interesting work and projects to do, and receive relevant job training. You would probably also attend short 'soft skills' training courses on topics like team building and leadership. Salaries are currently between £8000 and £12,000, but companies may pay more, especially if you were living away from home. If you wanted to enrol on this programme and also travel in your gap year, you could do both, as YINI contracts are usually around ten months. YINI in fact has a link with Madventurer (www.madventurer.com) under which students who complete their placement receive a 20% discount on any Madventurer expedition, many of which are five-week expeditions that take place in July and August. (www.yini.org.uk)

■ an Army short-service limited commission. (You would actually work as a junior officer.) The Army offers gap-year commissions that enable school leavers to take a short commission in the Army before attending university. There is no subsequent obligation to serve in the Army, but applicants must have a definite offer of a place on a degree course. (Competition is fierce.)

■ work in a leisure centre – and take the opportunity to gain coaching qualifications or qualify as a fitness instructor

■ work as a classroom assistant, or assistant matron in a private school, or in a children's holiday activity centre – this would be useful experience for intending teachers

■ taking a course in IT or secretarial skills/office administration – not only would you be able to take lecture notes and word-process your essays and assignments more quickly, but you should be able to find better paid part-time and vacation work as a student

■ doing a Teaching English as a Foreign Language (TEFL) qualification – this could lead to paid and voluntary holiday jobs abroad, and also to work in this country, teaching on Easter and summer holiday language courses for foreign students

■ qualifying as a fitness teacher, sports coach or aerobics instructor – again, you could find term-time and holiday work

■ getting qualifications in individual sports – you could then work as instructor in summer day and residential camps for children, in the UK and overseas.

Paid work overseas

Finding paid work overseas is not always easy, but jobs in hotels, restaurants and ski resorts are always quite easy to find. Gap-year students have worked in jobs as different as looking after children, crewing on boats, picking grapes, planting trees in Canada and herding sheep. Or how about:

■ working with American children in a summer camp

- au pair work in the USA or in Europe if you want to improve language skills? (You would be provided with food, accommodation, pocket money and helped to find language classes if appropriate.)

If you have a definite offer of a higher education place you can also apply to an organisation like BUNAC which can arrange paid work in North America and Australia.

Travel

The possibilities are almost endless, from a brief stay at a summer camp to having a back-packing year. The latter comes expensive though. You need sufficient funds to cover travel, living expenses and insurance. Some people do this now: others do it after graduation.

A good gap year could combine several of the above aspects.

Other ideas are in the books listed at the end of the chapter.

Going abroad? The boring bit

This covers some practical information that is far less exciting than working out what you are going to and where – but it could be tragic if you ignore it.

You can find a lot more information on the various gap-year websites and in the excellent books written for prospective gappers (see Chapter eleven). If you are planning to work on a voluntary project, the organisation that sends you will give you advice and make some of the arrangements for you. So – briefly you need to organise the following.

Equipment

Depending of course on where you are going, you might need any or all of the following items:

- good, strong backpack (with padlock)
- separate padlock (your insurance probably won't cover you if you

have property stolen from an unlocked room in a hostel)

- medical and first aid kit – visit your doctor's surgery or a high street pharmacy to see what's on offer (you can get ones that include an emergency dental repair kit and a set of needles and hypodermics – for transfusions or injections in places where the hygiene might be suspect)

- good quality boots

- sleeping bag

- mosquito net, preferably impregnated with repellent

- as little clothing as you can get away with – you can wash as you go.

That's a pretty basic list, and if you look in some sources of information you will see that you can get into all sorts of other things like water-sterilising equipment and jungle clothing. If you are going to spend the year in Italy or the USA then much of the above won't be relevant.

Flexible plane ticket

Don't go for the cheapest round-the-world fare. You get what you pay for. Pay a bit more and you will find that you are allowed to change timings, routes and even destinations if your plans change.

Source of emergency finance

Let's hope that this doesn't happen to you. One traveller last year was robbed while on a local bus in South America. The muggers who boarded the bus with guns, in the hope of fleecing locals, must have thought Christmas had come when they found him – plus cash, credit cards, camera and iPod. He was left with nothing, but managed to contact his travel insurer's helpline. They immediately cancelled all his cards and forwarded a pre-agreed amount of cash to the nearest bank. Their agent in the country then helped him to get to the nearest British Embassy to apply for a replacement passport.

Insurance

This is not to be skimped on. In addition to cover for emergencies like the one described above, you need cover for the following.

- *Cancellation or curtailment.* Suppose you have to fly home mid trip because of a family emergency. Or even worse, have some kind of accident and can't even go in the first place? With insurance cover you should get back some of the money you have paid out for travel tickets. The amount will depend on the proportion of the initial outlay that is unused.

- *Luggage and personal belongings.* You may not be going to take very much of value with you – but make a list and see if it adds up.

- *Medical expenses.* In most countries outside the UK you will have to pay for *all* medical treatment, and if your travels include the USA, the bill can be astronomical. A good policy will also cover the cost of emergency repatriation – even to the extent of providing you with an air ambulance and accompanying nurse.

- *Personal accident.* To provide compensation if you suffer the loss of a limb, for example.

- Then there are things like *personal liability.* To cover you if you cause damage to someone else or to their property.

- *Insurance cover for adventurous activities.* Most policies don't automatically cover hazardous sports.

However, don't worry. An industry has grown up to provide insurance for gappers and backpackers. You will be able to find a suitable one.

Unfortunately, all these boring costs can add up to lot more than you might think!

Useful books and websites

Books

■ *Taking a Year Off,* published by Trotman Publishing

■ *Making the Most of Your Gap Year,* published by Trotman Publishing

■ *A Year Off...A Year On?,* published by Lifetime Careers Publishing

Websites

Here are just a few examples of websites you can look at – some are examples of gap year opportunity providers; others carry information about a wide range of providers, and useful advice.

■ www.btcv.org

■ www.csv.org.uk

■ www.nationaltrust.org.uk/volunteering www.gapyear.com

■ www.yini.org.uk

■ www.gapyear.com – this site contains ideas, good advice and a message board for keeping in touch with other travellers

■ www.gapadvice.org – this site has tips, advice for people getting ready to travel and regular news bulletins

■ www.gap.org.uk – this is mainly for unusual and challenging projects

■ www.yearoutgroup.org – this covers an umbrella group of year-out organisations and lists gap year information events taking place in the UK.

Case studies

Joe

Community Service Volunteer

Joe, who is 19 and has A levels in biology, politics and psychology, is hoping to go to university to study politics. He has, however, already spent six months at an Oxford college – as a CSV volunteer. He spent that time supporting an 18-year-old first year Oxford student who has spastic diplegia and visual disabilities.

'I had decided to take a gap year after A levels, so have not made a UCAS application yet. That comes now. Earlier in the year I had cut out a small advertisement from CSV in _The Guardian_, and stuck it on my wall. I then more or less forgot about it until I needed to make some arrangements after the exam results.

I phoned CSV and received an information pack and application form. I filled the form in and sent it off – then was invited to an interview. It was very informal and designed to find out what kind of project I would be suited to. I didn't know what I wanted to do but I didn't rule anything out. I was then offered the Oxford placement as a personal helper to the student – who was studying history and politics.

Several of my friends wondered why I was doing this. They couldn't believe that I was having a gap year but not going to spend the time abroad backpacking. I actually spent six months working to earn some money and spent the other six moths on the project.

I was basically his live-in helper. The work was varied – some of it quite physical, like helping him to get up and to go to bed. I also had to give him one hour of physiotherapy each day, which I had been shown how to do. As his muscles were wasted it was important to prevent them from stiffening up and to keep them flexible.

Making sure that he had everything that he would need for his studies and making it possible for him to experience the social aspects of college life were important aspects of my job. I also spent a lot of time acquiring books and sorting out the notes that he needed to be working from. A lot of the resources he needed were useless to him because the size of the print was so small, so I spent some time photocopying the relevant sections to a viewable size. With the amount of reading he had to do, I spent a large proportion of my time in the copying room or getting books from libraries.

I had a room in the college quite near to him and all my meals were provided there. I also had an allowance from CSV which went on Oxford social life. I worked from Monday to Friday and staff from an agency came in to help him at weekends.

I attended lectures with him and really enjoyed the politics ones – although not so much the history. I didn't go to the one-to-one tutorials he had under the Oxford system though. That would have been rather intrusive. I was in an interesting position – not officially a student, but I felt like one and was accepted by everyone.

If you asked me what I got out of the experience I wouldn't say that I found out anything about myself that I didn't already know but I really enjoyed myself and had a good time. I made many new friends with whom I have kept in contact with and still see regularly. It was an opportunity that I have appreciated. I don't think there's another way in which I could have experienced that aspect of college life.'

Bonnie

Spent time as a volunteer in an orphanage in Central America

'I had to raise money towards the cost of my airfare and accommodation. But I also had to spend quite a bit on personal items. I had no idea until I started to shop just how much things like good boots and a rucksack cost. (They were for travelling at the end of the project.) I also had to pay for some of my injections. It was advisable to have a lot – rabies, yellow fever, hepatitis A, not to mention the more ordinary ones like typhoid, polio and tetanus.

I worked in a centre that housed abandoned or orphaned children; some with mental or physical handicaps. I worked with two other British volunteers and three South American ones. We all helped with all the chores, but it was rather sexist in that to begin with we girls did the cooking and the boys did maintenance work and work in the fields and the garden. After a while we began to change around and do all kinds of things. We each looked after one particular child. I looked after a little girl who had been brought in by a priest and had obviously been badly treated but wouldn't speak at all. I played games with her, sat with her at mealtimes and gradually coaxed her to eat properly with a spoon and fork. When she first came she simply grabbed food and swallowed it quickly, as though she was afraid that it would be taken from her. The children ranged in age from two to 15, so there was quite an age range to learn to communicate with. I also had to learn some Spanish pretty quickly in order to communicate with the children, the local volunteers and the full-time staff. I had a few lessons before I went, but I couldn't understand very much at first. I had a lot of help from one of the other English volunteers who had done A level and taught me a lot of useful phrases. I used these every day and gradually became more confident in speaking. One day I just decided that I had to communicate in Spanish from then on. People laughed at my mistakes – but nicely – and I am pretty fluent now.

I became good friends with the other British volunteers and we spent five weeks at the end of the placement travelling together – right down through South America and then up to Peru and Machu Picchu.

I had applied to do a degree in politics, but as a result of the gap placement I think that I might like to go into some kind of development or social work. I have changed to economics with Spanish. If I can, I will go back to work somewhere in Central or South America.'

Chapter nine
Making your decision

So – you have had quite a lot of (possibly too much) information. Now you have to do something with it – and that is to make a decision about your future. The first decision that is. It's time to start thinking about what you want to do for the next few years. You will have lots of opportunities, and maybe even the necessity to change track if the first plan doesn't work out.

Is a degree right for you? Does it fit in with your chosen career? Would you rather be getting your hands dirty and getting to the job market quicker? What about an HND? Or a gap year?

Armed with the knowledge you now have, try this simple quiz.

Your decision – quiz

1. What are your plans for the future?

1. I want to get a job as quickly as I can with a qualification specifically related to it.

2. I want to carry on in higher education and gain a Master's degree or a PhD.

3. I want to see some of the world and think about university later.

2. How would you like to train?

1. I like to get my hands dirty and get in some good practical work as well as some classroom based study.

2. I prefer theory work. I would rather learn lots at university and then apply my knowledge and gain experience when I'm actually working.

3. I've had enough of study for a while. I need a break.

3. What are your priorities as regards money?

1. I don't like debt.

2. I don't mind borrowing to invest in my future.

3. I'd rather enjoy myself for a while and get serious about it later.

4. How long would you be prepared to spend in getting some qualifications?

1. Three or four years.

2. Two years at the most, and only if I can study part time.

3. I want a while to think about it.

5. What kind of course were you planning on taking?

1. Something I can do while in employment – perhaps beauty therapy, business or childhood studies.

2. A traditional subject like English, maths, history, or a language.

3. None just yet.

6. What is your time scale?

1. I want to get started and settled in a career as soon as possible.

2. I want to improve my career prospects but keep my options open.

3. I'll want to get straight on with training when I graduate, so I need some *me* time now.

Done the quiz?

Well, it won't have taken you long to realise that the (a) answers were leading you towards a job or Apprenticeship, the (b) answers to full-time higher education, and the (c) answers to a gap year. But decisions are rarely as simple as this. There are no scores for this quiz – because there are no cut and dried answers and many people might not get straight (a) or straight (c) answers. There will be all sorts of factors to take into account. There is often more than one way of getting to the same goal. You could choose to do one, two or three of the available alternatives – and in various orders.

Influences

Ask for all the advice and help that you need.

What you need to do now is consult some or all of the people who were mentioned in Chapter five, plus any others you can think of. You will have decided by now which ones you find the most helpful, and which ones you wouldn't listen to at all. Ask their advice. Take it all in and weigh it up carefully. Read and research all the alternatives. Make lists of 'fors' and 'againsts' for each option if it helps. Then – think, think and rethink. Finally, thank everyone for their help *and do what you want to do. It's your decision.*

Summarising the alternatives

Higher education

Ask yourself these questions.

- Would you prefer a full-time or part-time course?
- Would you prefer a vocational or academic programme?
- Or a combination of both academic and vocational subjects?
- If you have decided on a vocational programme have you looked into Higher National Diplomas and foundation degrees?
- Have you checked the possibility of industrial sponsorship?
- Have you compared courses at different places?
- Would you like to stay at home?
- Or move away?
- Have you worked out approximate costs (as far as you can) and are you happy about the sources of finance open to you?

Work-related training

Ask yourself:

- Do you know what you want to do?
- Have you completed a computerised career choice program?
- Have you had or arranged a careers interview?
- Are you sure that the career you want to do can be entered by this route?
- Have you asked advice about Apprenticeships and other training schemes available in your area?
- Do you know what the pay would be?
- Have you discussed budgets with your parents – i.e. what contribution would you make towards your living expenses?

Gap year

Ask yourself:

- Have you made any definite plans?

- Can you afford to finance them?

- Do you need to spend a gap year earning money to help to finance your higher education?

- Will you spend the time, or some of it, abroad?

- If so, have you checked the various gap-year organisations carefully?

- Do you fully understand travel insurance and how much you might need to pay for it?

Good reasons for choosing a particular route

- It is something *you* want to do.

- There is a subject you really want to study, so higher education is the choice.

- You want to experience student life.

- There are several routes to the qualification you want and the quickest is by first taking a full-time course. You've weighed up the financial implications.

- There are several routes to the qualification you want, and you've weighed up the financial implications. You don't want to stack up a huge debt – so will do a longer, part-time route.

- You'd perform much better in a 'learning while earning' environment.

Bad ones...

- Everyone says you should do x.

- You want to go where your best friend is going.

- You think a particular course would be 'useful' but won't enjoy it.

- All your friends are going to uni so you might as well do so too.

- You've heard that Joe Bloggs' company is a good place to work. Well, it must be true, mustn't it?

- Your must-haves are x, y, z, ... and you'll never be able to afford them if you become a full-time student, so you'll go for the highest paid job you can find.

- It's not cool to do x or y.

- You don't know what the alternatives are – and make a lucky (?) dip.

Last (but not least)

Suppose you get it wrong? Suppose you choose a route now – and later decide you have made a mistake? 'Wrong' is a tough word. A decision, once made, isn't set in stone. OK, it would be nice to get it right the first time and stay in the job of your dreams until you retire – but life isn't like that! Luckily, education and training routes are so flexible nowadays that if you want to change career direction you can. In fact, many people will have several jobs during their lifetime. The reasons could be various – illness followed by inability to continue in their present job, redundancy, a feeling of time for a change, a change in domestic circumstances, and so on. People in these positions will have to rethink and change career direction. If you decided that you were a square peg in a round hole – you would have the same options open to you.

The following people all changed direction.

Sean

Sean couldn't wait to leave school at 18. All he wanted to do was work in order to earn enough money to survive while he trained hard in distance running. He hoped to be good enough for the Olympics. So he left with two A levels (biology and English) and took a series of temporary jobs. His parents supported his ambition, drove him to meetings all over the country, and helped out financially by letting him live at home without paying anything towards his food or keep. Fourteen years on he has a degree in sport science and works as a sports development officer, encouraging people in the local community to participate in sporting activities. He helps to set up voluntary groups and clubs, and coaches young people in athletics. (He didn't make the Olympic squad, incidentally, but he doesn't regret trying.)

What happened to change his mind? 'I saw the end of competitive running coming – and I was in a dead-end factory job. I had a lifetime of routine work and low earnings ahead of me. So I made enquiries at my local university – and was advised to take a GCSE or A level subject at evening class in order to get my brain going again. The college actually offered a 'Return to study' course, so I enrolled on that in addition to an A level in psychology. I was able to do this on one day each week – and I found a job in a sports equipment shop, working from Tuesday to Saturday. I was very popular because I was willing to work every Saturday!'

By now Sean had a partner – who was working. When he came to make his UCAS application, he could only apply to local universities and colleges. 'We had a mortgage by then, and were settled in the area.

There were only three mature students on the course and I was the oldest. To be honest, I didn't really notice. I was a local student with my own life, so although I got on well with all the group I didn't socialise much with the others. The 18-year-olds did strike me as immature though! They didn't seem to see the same need to work hard that I did. I suppose I was more motivated and was making more sacrifices to do the course.'

Beth

Beth, has a degree in history and now works in public relations.

'I left school with A levels and did a secretarial course. I had no interest in higher education. After a few years I got married and as my husband was in the Army we moved house every two years or so, and I couldn't think about doing any courses anyway. I also had two small children to look after. It was only when he decided to leave the Army – and started to think about retraining that I did the same. I could have easily found administrative jobs with my background, but I now decided on something different. I would do a subject that I enjoyed. If it didn't lead to a good job I could become a secretary again.

About a third of the students on my course were mature, but all ages worked well together on assignments and in study groups. The noticeable difference was that we older students were around during the day. Many of us were tied to school hours and spent the day on campus. I treated the college day as a day at work – went in at 9am and worked between lectures until it was time to pick up my children. And, of course, nights out and a hectic social life weren't for us.

I needed to manage my time more than I would have done at 18. The level of academic work wasn't difficult, but there was a huge reading commitment. There was one particular assignment that was so time-consuming that I despaired of doing it, but in the end I got it done. I also realised, to be honest, that many of the younger students were balancing their time too, since they were working in part-time jobs.'

Michelle

Michelle has a first-class degree in law and is applying for pupillages (the last stage of training for a career as a barrister).

After A levels she trained as a nurse and spent 12 years working in the NHS. She then moved to a private hospital – where things went wrong. Her career change began when she represented herself at an employment tribunal. 'I couldn't afford a lawyer, so had to represent myself – and read up law in a university library.' She won, and the opposing barrister asked her afterwards if she had ever considered a legal career. Michelle subsequently enrolled on a five-year, part-time evening degree course in law. She went back to work in an NHS hospital in order to finance her studies.

How did she cope with a degree course while working? 'With a lot of help', she says. Her colleagues willingly changed shifts to allow her to keep the two university evenings free. 'I couldn't have done it without them', she says – nor without the scholarship I was awarded for the one-year, full-time course I had to do after my degree.' When she graduated she won a scholarship from one of the Inns of Court.

It's never too late to change direction!

Chapter ten
Now you've made your decision

Now that you have (hopefully) decided what to do as your next step, you will have to make some applications.

Work applications

The method will be the same whether you are applying for a job with training built into it, or through the Apprenticeship programme. (You would apply to individual employers for Apprenticeships – just as for jobs – although there is a suggestion that a move might be made towards a 'clearing house' for school leavers that would match prospective trainees to employers in a similar way to the application schemes that operate for higher education.) In some areas it is also possible to apply to a *training provider* which organises the training of

Apprentices with several different employers, and ask them to find an employer for you. (Ask you personal adviser or careers adviser about this.)

The steps are likely to include:

- completion of an application form
- an interview.

Application forms

Imagine a human resources officer in a busy company – or worse, a small business where the owner does not have much office back-up and has to deal with all the post personally, reading through dozens of replies to a job advertisement. The last thing they want to do is trawl through ones that are difficult to read, don't answer the questions fully, or leave some blank. Those are reasons for the form ending up in the wastepaper bin! Many people are put off by spelling mistakes too.

Application form tips

- If it is a paper-based form, make several photocopies. Practise on these until you are happy with the result. (Then take a copy of the final version and keep it, ready to read through before an interview.)

- If it is an internet application – either print off some copies for practice or do practice versions on the real thing and delete as you go. There is a danger here, however – that you might hit the 'Send' button by mistake and send an incomplete version!

- If any questions do not apply to you, don't just leave the answer space blank. Put 'Not applicable' instead. (This shows that you have seen and read the question, and have not simply missed it.)

- Check the form carefully before sending, and ask someone else to check it for you as well. They may spot simple errors that you have missed, and might even suggest some better answers if they think that you have been too modest in places!

Application forms are often more than simple forms asking for your personal details and educational background. They often contain nasty questions like 'Give examples of your ability to inspire and motivate other people', 'Describe how you have overcome any difficulties or problems', 'Describe a situation in which you demonstrated leadership' and 'Give examples of your teamwork skills'. There is usually a space of several lines for you to write your answers – which are like short essays – and take some thought.

CVs

If no application form is involved, you may be asked to send a CV (or curriculum vitae) with a covering letter. Some employers may ask for one; others may prefer to see a record of achievement or your Progress File. However, it is a good idea to have a CV ready just in case... There are several different layouts, including chronological, reverse chronological, skills-based or professional formats. Later in your career you might decide to produce a skills-based CV, or one that starts with your most recent employment and works backwards (since the company you are applying to will be more interested in your most recent responsibilities), but for a school or college leaver the chronological method is one of the easiest.

Here is an example of a CV that a school or college leaver might write.

Mary Smith
The Laurels
Main Street
Little Sticksville
Barsetshire DN2 1PR
01234 567 8910*

Date of birth   6 April, 19XX

Nationality   British

Education   St. Philip's Secondary School
New Lane
Dring
Barsetshire DN2 3QS

Dring Sixth Form College
Valley Road
Dring
Barsetshire DN2 6HJ

Qualifications achieved

200X

GCSE: English language (A), mathematics (B), art (A), double science (B,B), French (C), German (B), geography (B), history (A), technology (A).

200X

AS level: English (A), French (B), government and politics (B), mathematics (A).

Qualifications to be taken

200X

A level: English, French, government and politics.

Out-of-school activities

I am a keen member of the college drama society, and have taken an active part in productions, both on stage and behind the scenes. Last year I played the daughter in *An Inspector Calls*. We are currently rehearsing a production of Chaucer's *Canterbury Tales* in modern dress. I am not acting in this but am the prompter.

I do voluntary work on Wednesday afternoons, when I assist a teacher in a local primary school. I spend time helping a small group of children with their reading.

Employment experience
June 200X

I spent two weeks on a work experience placement organised by my school, at the town leisure centre. I helped to set up and dismantle equipment, cleaned the changing rooms and worked on reception where I took bookings and handled cash. I also spent two Saturday afternoons helping to run children's parties. The experience gave me customer awareness and improved my communication skills.

I have a job every Sunday in a hotel coffee shop, where I am learning more about customer service together with acquiring an insight into how one part of the hospitality business is organised.

Skills

I am learning to drive.
I have improved my spoken French through several exchanges with my French correspondent.

Interests

Sport – I play regularly at a local badminton club.
Theatre – I have an annual subscription to Dring Theatre and see most of the performances.

Referees

Dr T Wescott **
Principal
Dring Sixth Form College
Valley Road
Dring
Barsetshire DN2 6HJ

Ms PL Lawrence
Food and Beverage Manager
The Royal Hotel
The Market Square
Dring
Barsetshire DN2 2OR

* Always give the area code.
** Never give people's names as referees unless you have first asked their permission.

Ask whose name you should give as the school referee. Your school may prefer you to give the name of your personal tutor, of your head of year or the head teacher/principal. (Some schools ask you to give the principal's name even though you may feel that he or she does not know you. There is a reason for this. The principal's secretary, or someone else from the administrative staff, is likely to be in work during every day of the summer holidays – when a lot of reference requests are received. They will open the post and send the reference request to the most appropriate person to write it. If you give your form tutor's name the letter might languish in his or her pigeon hole until they next go in to check their mail!)

CV tips

■ Try to make your CV fit onto one side of A4 if you can. If you must use more, number the pages.

■ Leave space between sections.

■ Justify the text – i.e. have both margins straight.

There are more tips on compiling CVs on national careers/Connexions websites. Your own school/college/Connexions partnership/careers centre may also produce them.

Covering letter

The covering letter that goes with your CV does not need to be very long. It should not repeat what is in the CV but should say why you want the particular job – and briefly why you are suitable for it, drawing out one or two points from the CV.

Covering letter tips

■ If you use a wordprocessor to produce your letter, then use the same size/quality/colour of paper as you did for your CV. (Although if you decide to hand-write your letter, use white, unlined writing paper, and use a line guide underneath to help keep the lines straight.)

■ Use the correct forms of address and signature. 'Dear Sir/Madam' takes *Yours faithfully*. 'Dear Mr Smith' takes *Yours sincerely*. These forms matter to a lot of recruiters – particularly older ones.

■ Some people 'top and tail' their letters by hand – i.e. write in the name of the person the letter is written to and the *Yours* etc in their own handwriting. You can decide for yourself whether or not to do this.

You will find other advice on composing a CV and writing covering letters (including speculative ones) in *Jobs and Careers after A level and equivalent advanced qualifications,* published by Lifetime Careers Publishing.

The interview

People naturally (whatever they may claim) are nervous before interviews. After all, they hope to be selected for the job. A good interviewer, however, will always try to put you at your ease. They know that they won't see the best side of applicants if they are frozen by fear. Try to remember too, that an interview isn't totally one-sided. You are finding out more about the job and the company, just as the interviewer is discovering more about you. At the end of the interview you might not want the job! But assuming that you will do, how can you make the best impression?

Preparation

In advance

■ Find out all you can about the company – what it makes, or what services it provides – and so on.

■ Think about the questions you might be asked, and try to work out some possible replies. Have some questions of your own ready as well.

■ Find out exactly where the interview will take place and work out how to get there. If you will be using public transport remember that buses and trains can be unreliable. Don't aim for the one that would get you there just in time. If you will be driving build in time to find somewhere to park. (And take some loose change in case you have to use a public car park.)

■ If the exact location of the interview isn't made clear – there could be more than one building within a walk from main reception – phone and ask for details. If your letter says 'Please report to reception' then you are OK.

The night before

■ Get your clothes ready. It's best to make these fairly formal. If the dress code is very informal you will know what you can wear when you start work, but you can't afford to take risks now. Most interviewers will be impressed by trousers and a shirt – and a tie isn't a bad idea – or a skirt and blouse. If you have a jacket, that will look good – but a suit isn't necessary. Make sure that your clothes are clean and have no buttons missing, and that you can find the shoes, tie, scarf, bag etc, that you need. And clean your shoes too.

■ Find your exam certificates, record of achievement/relevant documents from your Progress File, and any other certificate that you have been asked to take and put them in a folder.

■ Re-read your application letter or form, so that you can remember what you put on it.

On the day

■ Leave home in plenty of time.

■ Take with you the company's telephone number. (If you are unavoidably delayed you will be able to ring and explain.)

During the interview

Do

■ Smile when you meet the interviewer. First impressions count.

■ Wait to be asked to sit down when you enter the interview room.

■ Look the interviewer in the eye. It may be a panel interview with more than one person. If so, reply to the person who asked you the question – but look at the others too from time to time, to include them in the conversation.

- Be prepared to talk about yourself and your interests. This may not always seem relevant, but the interviewer wants to get to know something about you – and see whether you will fit into the organisation. (These questions might also be asked to put you at your ease initially.)

- You may also want to ask the interviewer questions about the training provided and the business. Prepare some questions (preferably about the job and the training involved first, before you get on to perks and holidays!) and don't be afraid to ask about other things that may come up in the course of the interview. They need to make a good impression on you, as well as the other way around. They want to recruit good employees with potential.

Don't

- Don't oversleep and miss the bus or train.

- Don't wear jeans and a sweatshirt.

- Don't walk in carrying your morning's shopping. (Leave it somewhere.)

- Don't mumble your name when you meet the interviewer.

- Don't sit down until you have been asked to do so.

- Don't fidget.

- Don't look down at the floor.

- Don't answer questions too quickly. (Take time to think.)

- Don't answer just 'Yes' or 'No' to questions.

- Don't invent an answer if you don't know the correct one. (Far better to admit it.)

- Don't talk too much.

- Don't become angry or aggressive.

- Don't ask questions when you should already know the answer. For example, don't ask for information which is contained in the job description.

- Don't ask how much you will be paid and what the perks are as your first questions.

What sorts of questions can you expect to be asked?

No two interviews are the same. Interviewers and their techniques vary. But most will start by asking about your journey, then move on to simple questions about what you have been doing recently, and so on.

When you have had time to relax they might move on to:

- your education and your school

- your interests and hobbies

- school subjects – your likes and dislikes, your strengths and weaknesses

- exams and results

- why you want this particular job

- why you have applied to this particular company or organisation

- your personality – how you get on with people of your own age, and with people of all ages and backgrounds

- your career choices and ambitions

- any part-time work mentioned on your application form

- whether you would be prepared to move to other parts of the country for promotion.

Some large organisations hold recruitment days. In this case you would attend with a lot of other applicants and be expected to do group and individual tests. You could take written tests, designed to assess personality, aptitude or specific abilities like working with IT. You might also be asked to undertake group work with other applicants to see how you work within a team.

Examples of team group exercises include:

- doing a treasure hunt

- building a tower from LEGO pieces

- building a tower from a packet of drinking straws that will support a brick when completed

- reading through information regarding an accident which has left six people trapped in a cave and deciding how to rescue them, stating in which order people should be rescued

- looking at a number of problems in a manager's in-tray and putting them in order of priority

- planning a fun 'thank you' day for a company's clients, choosing from a list of activities that would please both those with families and single and married people, including some people with disabilities

- discussing a topic totally unrelated to the job – but which requires no preparation or previous knowledge

- solving a problem from pieces of information provided

- discussing the ideal layout of a new office block the company is intending to build.

The point about all of these exercises is that someone will be watching to see who contributes most, who does very little, who takes the lead, who is overbearing and so on.

You have been warned.

You might also be asked to give a short presentation to the rest of the group – to test your verbal skills.

There are whole books written on interview techniques. Some of them may be in your school or college careers library. And again you should find some help on careers websites.

Particularly useful books are:

- *Excel at Interviews*

- *CVs and Applications*

Plus videos:

- *Choices @18*

- *The Essential Interview Video*

all published by Lifetime Careers Publishing.

If you are lucky enough to be offered more than one job or Apprenticeship, you will have to think carefully before deciding which one to accept. It will be up to you to decide which one will be the most suitable.

One company's recruitment process

BAe Systems is a large organisation with sites up and down the country. In a normal year it recruits 1000 Advanced Apprentices across all its sites, 45 for business and the remainder for engineering. The majority of applicants are moving up from an Apprenticeship but some are recruited with level 3 qualifications. Getting a place on an Apprenticeship programme with this company takes some effort! The programme is well respected and Apprentices are paid on a starting salary of £11-12,000. As a result there are on average three applications for every place. 'It costs us around £45,000 over three years to train each Apprentice' says John Lee Male, Head of Learning and Development. 'Naturally we select very carefully.'

Selection methods vary slightly between sites but always include a battery of aptitude tests – in spatial awareness, verbal reasoning, maths, and sometimes in personal skills. Some sites use teamwork exercises. All applicants are asked to bring an example of something they have made in their own time or in a school project.

Higher education applications

UCAS is a word that you will get to know well… UCAS is the Universities and Colleges Admissions Service. Based in Cheltenham, it handles applications to 95% of full-time higher education first degree and Higher Diploma courses. (If a course you wish to apply to is not in the UCAS system the prospectus will tell you how to apply and how to get an application form.) UCAS itself no longer uses paper application forms. From September 2005 – that is for entry to courses starting in autumn 2006 – it has moved to an all online application system. This is known as 'ucasapply' and was already being used by an increasing number of applicants when there was still a choice of paper forms or web based application. Hiccups should have been removed from the system by now, and school and college staff new to the apply system have received training in its administration. So, they will tell you what to do and handle all the fine detail.

The advantages of the new system are as follows.

■ You can work on your application wherever you have access to the internet.

■ The onscreen instructions will guide you on how to complete the form and will remedy any mistakes (if you make any).

■ You can work on the application at different times and change it as often as you like before you pass the final version to the person who is going to add a reference about you and send the application in.

So – armed with the *UCAS Directory* which lists all the courses, and having done all your research, you need to select up to six courses. You list these on the application form, fill in all the other information required, pay your application fee (£15 for more than one course; £5 if applying to one course only) and off goes the application. The one course option is normally used only by applicants who have one very specific course and institution in mind – perhaps their local one. Most applicants use all six courses, but there is no compulsion to do so. You may send a UCAS application at any time after 1 September in the year ahead of entry, and are advised to have it in by the advisory closing date of 15 January. This is the ideal closing date because applications received after this date are regarded as late, and although UCAS will forward them to universities and colleges they are not obliged to consider them and might only do so if they expect to have some places unfilled. But – if there are reasons why someone cannot make an application at the usual time, they might be relieved to hear now that they are accepted right until the start of term in the following year.

There are some important exceptions.

- If you apply for medicine, dentistry, veterinary science or any course at all at Oxford or Cambridge there is an earlier closing date of 15 October.

- There are two methods of applying for degree courses in art and design. These are explained later.

There is a calendar showing crucial UCAS dates at the end of the chapter.

What happens to your UCAS application after it leaves you?

Staff at UCAS check it – and if they find any discrepancies they contact you. They then copy your form and send both paper and electronic copies to all the institutions you have listed. (The universities and colleges receive your form *minus* the names of the other ones you have chosen – so they have no means of knowing what other choices you have made.)

How quickly the next stage happens depends on how quickly the admissions tutors at each place can deal with the forms. They have until April to make their decisions on applicants, but most act far more quickly than that. Many applicants start to receive replies before Christmas. It can be very stressful when some students hear from institutions before others do. However, a gap between sending off your form and receiving a reply does not necessarily mean bad news. A lot depends on how many applications are made to a particular course, and how many people are dealing with the applications. They are read by members of full-time teaching staff who do the UCAS admissions work on top of their ordinary workload. So, try not to worry if friends are receiving replies before you do.

The decisions can be conditional offers, dependent on your getting certain exam grades, or unconditional ones if you already have the grades – or unfortunately, rejections. They can come at any time, but you do not have to reply to any of them until you are sent a final Statement of Decisions from UCAS. This will list all your offers and ask you to choose between them. It will also show a deadline for doing so. This will vary according to when the last university or college sent UCAS its decision.

You might or might not be invited to attend an interview before a selector for a course makes a decision. Interviews are not as common as they used to be, because of pressure on staff time – but are almost always held for:

- art and design – when you are expected to show some of your work

- courses that require vocational commitment – like medicine, nursing, teaching and social work.

You can check the progress of your application at any time using UCAS' online tracker service, which will be explained to you once UCAS has initially dealt with your application. You can also contact UCAS staff at any time – but it is important to understand that they merely operate the service. They do not make any decisions on your application.

When you have had replies from all your choices it is up to you to make decisions. You may accept just one offer firmly. This means that you are committed to going to that institution if it confirms that it has accepted you after the exam results. You may also accept one insurance offer. Students often wonder whether it is worth accepting the second offer. Yes it is. If you don't get the results you need for your first choice you will have somewhere to go – somewhere you have already decided that you like (as opposed to making a new choice at the last minute). It is important to put as much thought into accepting your insurance offer as for the firm one. You would be committed to it, just as that institution would have to honour its obligation to you.

UCAS Extra and Clearing

What happens if you do not receive any offers? Or if you change your mind about what you want to do, or where you would like to do it?

Getting six rejections feels like the end of the world. But there are all sorts of reasons for this happening. Some students apply for extremely popular courses. The competition is high – and someone has to lose out. Some apply only to the 'in' universities and colleges – where the same thing can happen. Others take a gamble. Their subjects or predicted grades aren't quite right for the course, but they decide to chance it.

If you did not receive any offers you would have two further chances to find a place. The first would be through a service known as UCAS Extra, which takes place between mid March and the end of June. UCAS staff would identify applicants who don't have any offers (including any who had declined all the ones they did receive) and would contact them. If you decided to use UCAS Extra you would be sent a 'Passport' with your personal number printed on it. Universities and colleges with vacant places would list them on the UCAS website. You would be able to look at them, check them out and make contact direct either by sending your Passport or by using the UCAS Applicant Enquiry Service.

If you ended up with no offers you would need to consider all the options. You could apply for the same course but at a new place. You could also increase your chances by searching for slightly different subjects or a wider range of universities and colleges. This needn't be too drastic (like changing from history of art to physics), you might consider changing to courses with similar content to those of your original choice (like literary studies instead of English, or modern history instead of general history). You could also look at joint courses which included a major amount of your original subject but meant that you would have to do something else with it.

You would need to take care using UCAS Extra, because it allows applicants to accept only one offer. You would need to ask for advice from someone at school, college or the careers/Connexions service and discuss whether it might be better to hang on and wait for the second service, Clearing, which takes place in August after the publication of the exam results.

At the end of the day there is no commitment. You don't have to accept offers through UCAS Extra. If no places really interest you, you can hang on and wait for Clearing. You've probably heard about Clearing. This service has been operated by UCAS for several years and helps thousands of students to find places. It is a much bigger version of UCAS Extra – with vacancies also advertised in the national press. Universities and colleges with vacant places notify them to UCAS, which produces Clearing lists, and also advertise them in the national press. Students without places in August can then get in contact and, hopefully, find places on suitable courses.

Art and design courses

There are two ways to apply for degree courses in art and design courses – Route A and Route B. If a course is listed as Route A in the *UCAS Handbook*, you must use Route A to apply for it. If a course is listed as Route B, you must use Route B.

For courses using Route A, the application method is exactly the same as for other UCAS courses – you can list up to six choices and your application would be sent to each of the universities or colleges at the same time.

Route B applicants have a different system. Their applications are *sequential* – i.e. go to their first choice only to begin with, and are only sent on to second and if necessary, third choices if they are not accepted earlier.

If you wanted to apply to the fine art course in Route A at the Ruskin School of Fine Art, Oxford, your form would have to reach UCAS by 15 October. You would also submit a portfolio of artwork by 15 November.

For courses using Route B, you can list up to three choices on the UCAS application. Forms must be received by UCAS between 1 January and 24 March, but it is advisable to apply by 7 March if possible.

Application forms are sent to applicants' first choice institutions, which decide whether or not to offer places. If applicants accept offers the process stops there. If they do not receive offers, or receive them but decline them, application forms go to your second choice, and third if necessary.

You could apply for courses through both Route A and Route B, but you must not choose more than three Route B courses. The following examples show the combinations of choices that are allowed.

■ 3 Route B choices + 3 Route A choices

■ 3 Route B choices + 2 Route A choices

■ 3 Route B choices + 1 Route A choice

■ 2 Route B choices + 4 Route A choices

■ 1 Route B choice + 5 Route A choices.

UCAS applications calendar

1 September

UCAS forms accepted from this date.

The earlier the better – admissions tutors start to make offers as they read application forms. They do *not* wait until the closing date. *But* don't rush. Take time to choose courses carefully.

15 October

Closing date for applications for medicine, dentistry, veterinary science and for any course at Oxford or Cambridge.

1 January

Art and design Route B applications now accepted.

You may have only three choices (but may make three more through Route A).

15 January

Closing date for applications – including art and design Route A.

You may still apply, but your form will be stamped 'Late' and universities and colleges will not be obliged to consider you.

7 March

Recommended deadline for art and design Route B applications.

Mid March to end of June

UCAS Extra will give applicants with no offers the opportunity to make an additional choice from places still available.

24 March

Art and design Route B applications received now will be considered late but will still be forwarded.

April

If you applied by 15 January for the main UCAS scheme (including art and design Route A) you should have received final decisions from all the colleges and universities you applied to.

You do not have to reply until UCAS sends you a *Statement of Decisions* with a reply slip. You may accept one offer *firmly* and one *insurance*. Think carefully, then complete the slip and return it to UCAS.

7 April

First round of art and design Route B interviews begins.

12 June

Route B applications received after this date will now have to wait until Clearing.

23 May

Second round of art and design Route B interviews begins.

12 June

Third round of art and design Route B applications begins.

30 June

All other forms, including art and design Route A, received after this date will go into Clearing.

July

If you applied between 16 January and 30 June for the main UCAS scheme (including art and design Route A) you should now receive final decisions.

CUKAS

CUKAS (Conservatoires UK Admissions Service) is a specialist service for students who wish to apply for practice-based music courses at the following institutions – Birmingham Conservatoire, Leeds College of Music, Royal College of Music, Royal Northern College of Music, Royal Scottish Academy of Music and Drama, Royal Welsh College of Music and Drama, and Trinity College of Music. This is a completely online service. You would apply by logging on to www.cukas.ac.uk – choosing a maximum of six courses and following the instructions there.

CUKAS dates are different from the main UCAS ones. You can apply from 3 May in the year ahead of entry and there is a closing date of 1 October – although later applications may be considered at institutions' discretion until 31 May.

Students are allowed to apply to six courses in the UCAS system as well.

Nursing Diplomas

Whereas applications for degree courses in nursing and midwifery are made through UCAS, Diploma level applications in England are handled by the Nursing and Midwifery Admissions Service (NMAS). The system works in a similar way to UCAS system *but* on paper-application forms and with different dates and deadlines.

Forms should be received at NMAS with the application fee (£12 for up to four choices, or £6 for a single choice) before 15 December. Late applications received between 16 December and 30 June will be forwarded to institutions for consideration, subject to vacancies remaining. Applications received after 30 June will not be processed.

All decisions will be sent to NMAS who will then notify the applicants. Like UCAS, NMAS operates a Clearing service. This runs from mid-June until September. Applicants who go into Clearing are sent a Clearing Entry Form (Passport) and a list of institutions and courses on which there are still vacancies. They then contact the institutions directly.

In Scotland the CATCH system (Centralised Applications (to nursing and midwifery) Training Clearing House) processes all applications for nursing Diploma courses. Applicants may choose four courses – and the process is sequential. Application forms are sent to the first choice and on to the others in order if the applicant is not accepted. Like the other centralised application systems, CATCH also runs a Clearing service.

Art and design foundation courses
(or level 3 Diplomas in foundation studies, art and design)

These courses are diagnostic courses that provide a bridge between the type of work done for A level and that on a Higher Diploma or degree course. They are held in art schools, universities and further education colleges. There is no central application system.

The closing date for applications varies from college to college. It is therefore important to find out when they are and be sure not to miss any.

The system in Scotland is slightly different: most degree courses are four years in length and include the equivalent of a foundation course. In some cases, students can enter the second year directly if they have undertaken a suitable foundation course.

Selection

How do higher education institutions select their students?

On the basis of the information on the application form, including:

- known examination results

- predicted grades in forthcoming examinations

- the reference(s)

- students' Personal Statements.

In some very competitive subjects universities may set additional admissions tests. They are common in law, medicine and veterinary science. The tests are designed to find whether applicants have the additional skills or aptitudes that are required for the course, and which are not necessarily tested by A levels. The medical one, for example, is designed to test thinking skills. Oxford and Cambridge Universities often set additional tests or ask to see examples of candidates' written work. Most other universities and most other subjects rely on exam grades alone or include an interview.

You can find information on entry tests at
www.ucas.com/test/index.html

Admissions tutors who read the application forms and make up their minds whether or not to offer places use the above criteria. In addition, many have their own likes and dislikes. It's common, for instance, for them to dislike spelling mistakes, poor grammar, misuse of the apostrophe – and a relatively new one – use of text language!

One admissions tutor who has long experience of selecting students says 'The more popular the course, the more factors will be considered.

- Are predicted grades consistent with GCSE grades?

- Are candidates focused in their selection of courses?

- Do the academic references modify points raised on the candidates' forms? Do they raise issues which may affect candidates' performance?

- Do personal statements justify course and university choice?

- Presentation is crucial. Spelling and grammar are important. I like to think that applicants have spent more time completing their forms than the appearance of some would suggest.'

Personal Statements

Nearly all applications forms give you a space to 'sell yourself' and explain why you would benefit from doing the course. The UCAS one may not contain more than 4000 characters, including spaces. Others vary from those that allow an A4 page, to others giving you only a few lines. Whichever type of form you are faced with it's important to do several drafts before hitting the button or posting the form.

Here again, there are some pet likes and dislikes. One tutor says 'My pet hates are comments such as 'I like reading' and 'I like socialising'. The first requires more detail – what sort of reading and why? The second suggests clubbing and pubbing – interests that are not seen as relevant to the chosen course!'

There is no one way to write a Personal Statement, but there is some general advice.

Using clear paragraphs or sections is a good idea. The first could explain why you are applying for the subject. Tutors like motivation. But avoid the opening 'History/English/maths is my favourite subject.' That's fairly obvious. Instead, try saying *what* you enjoy about it. What if you are applying for something new? Tell them that you have researched it and know what it involves.

Other paragraphs can be used for your interests and any part-time paid or voluntary work. Anything that demonstrates being consistent and managing your time looks good. These are important skills in an environment where you are very much responsible for your own work. So, you could write about the sports team that you give time to every weekend, or the time and effort you put into gaining a Duke of Edinburgh's Award.

How you describe such activities is important too. Rather than simply listing a page worth of interests – and make them wonder whether you ever stick at anything or find time for A-level work – you should try to draw out what you gain from them. So it's not good to say 'I do x, y and z…' Better is 'I am in an amateur drama group, which takes up several evenings a week when we are rehearsing a play. Being a member has increased my self-confidence and has taught me skills in working with other people. Currently we are working on…'

Phrases to avoid are the bland 'I read.' (Who doesn't?) and 'I enjoy socialising.'

An art foundation course application form could include:

■ reasons for wanting to study art

■ reason for choice of college

■ interest within art – areas of art that you enjoy, e.g. fashion, fine art, graphics

■ artists that inspire you, exhibitions that you have seen

■ future areas of specialisation – if known.

This is one science admissions tutor's preference.

'I like three sections.

■ The first should explain why you chose your course. This could be because it contains certain options, includes a sandwich placement…

■ Next, there should be some evidence that you are suitable for the course. If you are doing an A level in my subject I want to know what you enjoy about it. If my course is going to be a totally new area, I need you to tell me that you have researched it – and are not choosing it simply because you hate your A2 subjects! Then, I as a vocational course tutor, would like to see some indication of possible career plans.

- Finally, a section about yourself. This is the most difficult. Every admissions tutor likes to think that every student he or she accepts will be motivated and hardworking. We are all looking for evidence of commitment and the ability to stick at something over a period. So do write about the drama group you have been in for two years, or the fact that you worked for the same Saturday employer for two. Musical instrument grades show commitment too. What you have done is less important than what you have gained from it. Describe the team working or leadership skills you gained for instance.'

To sum up

Do

- Take all the advice you can get.

- Make several drafts.

- Think hard about the activities you put here. Use your Progress File/record of achievement, part-time employment, out of school interests.

Don't

- Don't just give a list of hobbies.

- Don't give too many. (You don't want tutors to think that you will have no time for academic work.)

- Don't list 'reading' and 'going to the cinema'. Who doesn't?

Extracts from two good Personal Statements

Applicant for a modern languages degree

'In addition to studying two languages for A-level, I am learning Russian at evening classes. The language is complicated and I have to fit in homework around my A2 work. However, I am persevering.

I have taken part in three exchange visits to France and Germany. All were spent at the home of my partner students, and on two I attended their schools with them. The third exchange was the most exciting because it included four days' work experience. I chose to work in a French town hall where I helped to process housing benefit information. This was the biggest challenge I have met.

Of the four language skills I particularly enjoy speaking, but I also like the analytical and written aspects of languages. I read widely, from poetry to contemporary fiction and books on certain aspects of European history. I am looking forward to studying French and Italian literature.

I have chosen to begin Italian as I want to learn a new language, and because I am interested in the Italian history that has been covered in my A level course. I want to study the Renaissance period in more depth and am also interested in the development of Italy since reunification.

My interests outside school include music and sport. I play the clarinet in a youth orchestra and swim and play tennis regularly. I also have a Sunday job in a fast-food outlet where I have developed my customer service skills and learned to work under pressure.'

Applicant for an English degree

'I have always taken a keen interest in English and love both the analytical and written aspects of the subject. I read widely, from poetry to contemporary fiction and books on certain aspects of European history. I also enjoy writing and in the future I hope to pursue a career in journalism.

Last year I approached the editor of the local paper and asked whether I could do any unpaid work experience over the summer holiday. I worked there for five weeks and graduated from making the tea and coffee and filing to writing some short articles, some of which were published. I learned a good deal there about how journalists have to work to tight deadlines, under pressure, and how everyone has to help out in other sections from time to time. I also saw the unglamorous sides of the work when I had to watch sports matches in freezing temperatures. I found visiting some court trials harrowing at first, but learned to cope. I still work at the paper's offices every Saturday and have to be very careful about fitting this around my A2 work.

My other main interest is art and design. I love painting, both still life and abstract. During a recent trip to Paris I was able to visit the Louvre and the Picasso Museum.

I voluntarily assist in a local primary school, working with small groups of children to complete various tasks which include arts and crafts, playing games and helping the children to improve their reading skills.

I have also had work experience in the legal department of a large company. This gave me the invaluable experience of working within a team.'

Interviews

The rules here are very similar to those for job interviews. Prepare thoroughly. Think of some questions that you might expect to be asked and work out some answers to them. Make a list of questions you can ask. Re-read your Personal Statement the day before the interview – and so on. You need not dress quite so formally, but otherwise follow the guidelines given earlier in the chapter. You can expect to be asked to expand on what you wrote on the application form, and you can expect to be asked about your present subjects. At an interview for a vocational course be ready to talk about your commitment, work experience and so on.

Good luck!

Chapter eleven
Sources of information

In order to make the right decision, you will need to gather together plenty of information so that you can make a well-researched choice. Hopefully you have read Chapter five and found it helpful. There are many useful sources listed there and suggestions too of people who should be able to assist you.

This chapter contains a list of the useful websites, books and videos that you can consult. You should be able to find most of them in a school or college careers resources room or library.

General careers information

If you would like more details about what particular jobs entail before you make your career or higher education choice, look at websites and general careers books such as the following.

Websites

Careers Scotland – www.careers-scotland.org.uk

Careers Wales – www.careerswales.com

National Connexions website – www.connexions.gov.uk

Connexions Direct website (for web chat or emailing an adviser)– www.connexions-direct.com

Connexions Direct careers information (your local Connexions site) – www.connexions-direct.com/jobs4u

Apprenticeships, England – www.apprenticeships.org.uk

Apprenticeships, Scotland – www.scottish-enterprise.com

Apprenticeships, Northern Ireland – www.delni.gov.uk

Apprenticeships, Wales – www.elwa.ac.uk

National jobs and training site – www.worktrain.gov.uk

Sector Skills Councils– www.ssda.org.uk

Books

Careers 2006, published by Trotman Publishing (A directory of general careers information containing information on specific occupations.)

Job Book, published by Hobsons Publishing (Contains information on employers and the job opportunities they offer.)

What Do Graduates Do? published by UCAS/CSU/AGCAS (Contains details of the employment destinations of UK graduates under several different subject headings.)

CVs and Applications, published by Lifetime Careers Publishing

Excel at Interviews, published by Lifetime Careers Publishing

Jobs and Careers After A levels and Equivalent Advanced Qualifications, published by Lifetime Careers Publishing

You Want to Do What?!, published by Trotman Publishing (80 alternative career options.)

Videos

Choices @ 18 video – it's your life, published by Lifetime Careers Publishing

The Essential Interview Video, published by Lifetime Careers Publishing

N.B. Be sure to consult the latest and most up-to-date editions of all the above. (Look for the publication date on the cover or front page.)

You could also visit a careers fair or convention. Sometimes a school, a group of schools or a local careers or Connexions service arranges a careers day or evening at which colleges and large employers – such as the Armed Forces, banks, the Health Service and major local companies – set up stands and provide representatives who are willing to answer questions. As with higher education fairs referred to in Chapter five it pays to decide beforehand who you want to see and what you need to ask.

Higher education

Websites

Department for Education and Skills – www.dfes.gov.uk/hegateway

Study in Scotland – www.studyinscotland.org

Quality Assurance Agency for Higher Education – www.qaa.ac.uk/students

QAA subject reviews – www.qaa.ac.uk/reviews

QAA course content – www. qaa.ac.uk/academic infrastructure/ programspec

Teaching Quality Information – www.tqi.ac.uk

National Student Survey – www.thestudentsurvey.com

Edexcel – www.edexcel.org.uk

Foundation degrees – www.foundationdegree.org.uk

UCAS – www.ucas.com

USAS, information on entry tests – www.ucas.com/test/index.html

Find the right subject – www.ukcoursefinder.com

Advice and lifestyle – www.studentuk.com

Books

CRAC Degree Course Guides, published by Trotman Publishing (20 different subjects.)

CRAC Which Degree Guide, published by Careers Research Advisory Centre

Degree Course Offers, published by Trotman Publishing

Directory of University and College Entry, published by Trotman Publishing (Lists foundation degree plus Diploma courses in subjects including art and design, drama and music, in addition to the better-known degree, HND and Dip HE courses.)

How to Read League Tables, published by UCAS

The Student Book, published by Trotman Publishing

The UCAS Directory, published by UCAS

University and College Entrance – The Official Guide, published by UCAS

The UCAS/Universities Scotland Entrance Guide to Higher Education in Scotland, published by UCAS

The Virgin Alternative Guide to British Universities, published by Virgin Books

Trotman's Green Guides (published by Trotman):

- *Art, Design and Performing Arts Courses*
- *Business Courses*
- *Engineering Courses*
- *Healthcare Courses*
- *Physical Sciences Courses*

If you have special needs

Into Higher Education, published by Skill (National Bureau for Students with Disabilities)

Skill Information Sheets, published by Skill (National Bureau for Students with Disabilities)

Applications

CATCH
PO Box 21
Edinburgh EH2 2Y
Tel: 0131 220 8660
www.nes.scot.nhs.uk

NMAS
Rosehill
New Barn Lane
Cheltenham
Gloucestershire GL52 3LZ
Tel: 0870 112 2206
www.nmas.ac.uk

UCAS
Rosehill
New Barn Lane
Cheltenham
Gloucestershire GL52 3LZ
Tel: 0870 112 2200
www.ucas.com

Student finance

Websites

England and Wales, DfES website –
www.dfes.gov.uk/studentsupport

Northern Ireland, Education and Library Boards:

Belfast – www.belb.org.uk

North Eastern – www.neelb.org.uk

South Eastern – www.seelb.org.uk

Southern Education – www.selb.org.uk

Scotland – www.saas.gov.uk

For student funding and awards – www.scholarship-search.org.uk

Tips and advice from HE students – www.interstudent.co.uk/channel_money.php

For students leaving care – www.doh.gov.uk/surviveoutthere/index.htm

For students with disabilities, the National Bureau for Students with Disabilities – www.skill.org.uk

Books

The Grants Register, published by Macmillan

Educational Grants Directory, published by the Directory of Social Change

A Guide to University Scholarships and Awards, published by Trotman Publishing

Sponsorship and Funding Directory, published by Hobsons Publishing

Student Life: A Survival Guide, published by Lifetime Careers Publishing

Students' Money Matters, published by Trotman Publishing

Surviving on a Shoestring, published by Trotman Publishing

For courses in subjects related to medicine

Department of Health
PO Box 777
London SE1 6XH
Email: doh@prolog.uk.com
Website: www.doh.gov.uk/hcsmain.htm

Or enquiries may be directed, if you plan to study in England, to:

NHS Student Grants Unit
22 Plymouth Road
Blackpool
Lancashire FY3 7JS

Tel: 01253 655655
Email: enquiries@nhspa.gov.uk
Website: www.nhspa.gov.uk

In Northern Ireland:

North Eastern Education and Library Board
County Hall
182 Galgorm Road
Ballymena
County Antrim BT42 1HN
Tel: 028 2565 3333
Website: www.neelb.org.uk

In Scotland:

The Students Awards Agency for Scotland
Gyle View House
3 Redheughs Rigg
South Gyle
Edinburgh EH12 9HH
Tel: 0845 111 1711

In Wales:

NHS Wales Students Awards Unit
2nd Floor Golate House
101 St Mary Street
Tel: 029 2026 1499
Email: sau@hpw.org.uk

Gap year

European Voluntary Service
Connect Youth International
British Council
Spring Gardens
London SW1A 2BN
Tel: 020 7389 4030
Website: www.britishcouncil.org

Websites

Here are just a few examples of websites you can look at – some are gap year opportunity providers; other websites carry links and information about a wide range of providers, and useful advice.

- www.btcv.org

- www.csv.org.uk

- www.nationaltrust.org.uk/volunteering

- www.gapyear.com

- www.yini.org.uk

- www.gapadvice.org (This site has tips, advice for people getting ready to travel and regular news bulletins.)

- www.gap.org.uk (This is mainly for unusual and challenging projects.)

- www.gapwork.com

- www.gapyear.com

- www.intervol.org.ul (International volunteering)

- www.yearoutgroup.org (This covers an umbrella group of year out organisations and lists gap year information events taking place in the UK.)

- www.shell-livewire.org

- www.trekforce.org.uk (Trekforce expeditions)

- www.vacationwork.co.uk

Books

A Year Off… A Year On? Published by Lifetime Careers Publishing

Making the Most of Your Gap Year? Published by Trotman Publishing

Opportunities in the Gap Year? Published by ISCO Publications

What Do Graduates Do? Published by UCAS

Sponsorship and Funding Directory? Published by Hobsons Publishing

Summer Jobs Abroad? Published by Vacation Work Publications

Summer Jobs in Britain? Published by Vacation Work Publications

Taking a Gap Year? Published by Vacation Work Publications

Taking A Year Off? Published by Trotman Publishing

Work Your Way Around the World? Published by Vacation Work Publications

Working Holidays Abroad? Published by Trotman Publishing

(There are many other websites and books on gap years. Above is just a selection to give you an idea of the range of available resources.)

Index